Willis Stories

Volume 2

Third Edition

by

Keith M Willis

ISBN: 9798863688497

Uncle Harv

Harv Jensen was my mom's brother. I remember him as a good guy with a good family. He always treated me well. A few years ago, before Harv passed away, two of my cousins made a video of Harv recounting some of his wartime experiences. Harv was a career military pilot who flew in all of the wars from World War 2 through Vietnam. During the video he was asked to pick his most harrowing combat experience, whereupon he looked at my cousins and asked, "Just one?"

So he related a flight he made over Japan near the end of WW2 where his plane was strafed by ground fire. He ended up in a small raft in the ocean paddling away from the Japanese mainland. He was later picked up by a U. S. ship.

When I was young, Harv told me several wartime stories. One incident happened either in WW2 or Korea. Allied ground troops needed a bomb dropped on a specific location that was difficult for planes to target. There were surrounding hills and cliffs, and the target site was at the base of one of those cliffs. Air Command was asked to send one of their best pilots because the location of the target was problematic.

Harv got the task and he told me that when he made his bomb run, he was focused mainly on the small target. He aimed and dropped his bomb, then looked up, and saw that he was about to die. Rushing straight at him was a cliff wall of granite. Immediately he pulled back on the plane's control stick as hard as he could. Then he blacked out. His plane barely cleared the mountain top.

5

When he awoke seconds later, he remembered what had happened and now had to regain control of the airplane. First, he looked around for the ground. Then it was a matter of moving the control stick and adding thrust to right the aircraft.

Another close call that Harv shared with me also happened either in WW2 or Korea. His plane had been hit and was on fire so he radioed a "Mayday" and headed for a landing zone. He set his plane on the ground, shut down the engines, and taxied to a stop. Popping the canopy, he made a jump and ran for safety, but he forgot about being tethered to the airplane. His flight suit had a cord attached to a parachute. The cord tripped him and he broke his ankle. I don't remember whether his plane blew up or not.

Harvey Jensen - Pilot - South Korea

Some years later Harv worked at the Pentagon and shared a desk there with a marine pilot named John Glenn. He and John became friends. When John Glenn joined NASA to become an astronaut, Harv took over John's Pentagon tasks. John Glenn became the first American to orbit the Earth. Harv met other NASA astronauts as well as Vice President Lyndon Johnson through his friendship with John Glenn.

Patti Skis

Uncle Harv told me a story years ago when I visited him and Aunt Joyce in Dana Point, California. Uncle Harv and Aunt Joyce had two children, Rick and Patti, and they did some boating as a family growing up. All of them became good water skiers.

When I asked about his kids, Uncle Harv told me a fun story about Patti. She was in her twenties then and she went to a party somewhere with a bunch of friends or classmates. It was at a lake and everybody brought swimwear. There was a boat and some of the boys were water skiing. Patti was sunbathing.

After awhile Patti asked if she could ski, and this is when Uncle Harv began to smile. He told me the boys were surprised that one of the girls could water ski. Of course they would let her ski. They backed the boat toward the shore, threw her the tow rope, and tossed her two skis. She pushed one of the skis back to the boat, telling them she would be fine with one ski. She was standing in 18 inches of water when she slipped the slalom ski on.

She waved for the boat to go and off they went. Patti stood up on the slalom ski and began doing cuts and curves and spraying wake as the boat circled the lake. After several trips around the lake, Patti waved to the boat driver that she was done. The driver buzzed the lake shore where they started. Patti let go of the rope and skied to the shore on one ski. Then she stepped off into 18 inches of water and tossed the ski back to the boaters.

When she walked back to her lounge chair, the girls were speechless. The boys were impressed. Her bathing suit wasn't even wet after skiing around the lake. Uncle Harv was laughing by now.

Pet Squirrel

My youngest brother, Wayne, was walking home from middle school one day with a friend and they found an abandoned baby squirrel on the ground. They took it to the friend's house and put it in a large birdcage. The friend fed the little squirrel and it began to grow. When the friend's family went on vacation, the birdcage and squirrel came to our house for babysitting and feeding.

Everybody in both families loved the little animal. He wasn't afraid of people and ran freely around the house. We all fed him and he was always looking for a food handout. If somebody opened a bag of chips or snacks, the crackling of paper brought him like a magnet.

As the squirrel grew larger, his sharp claws became a problem for furniture and curtains. He would crawl up people's legs and jump onto their shoulders, and his sharp claws could be painful. When he heard people coming to the front door of our home, he would run and jump onto the inside screen of the front door to see who was there. The mailman complained to my mother about the scary animal living inside our house.

When the squirrel reached full size, Wayne's friend released him outdoors. The squirrel quickly blended in with other tree squirrels in the area, but he didn't stray far from our house. If he saw people on the ground that he recognized, he would climb down a tree and come begging for food on the ground.

My youngest sister, Angela, was about five years old then and she loved that little squirrel. She fed him and played with him and talked to him. One day she was in our backyard and the squirrel came down from the trees to visit her. Our senior neighbor next door was in his backyard and the squirrel went over to visit him and beg for food. The neighbor didn't know the squirrel was a pet, so when the squirrel walked up to him and grabbed his pant leg with his teeth, the neighbor thought the animal might have rabies. He grabbed a shovel nearby and chopped the little squirrel in half. My little sister witnessed this and let out a scream. My mom came running out of the house and ran to the neighbor's house and told him the squirrel was a neighborhood pet. The neighbor was shocked at what he'd done.

After that day, none of the Willises could ever talk about the squirrel or the neighbor in Angie's presence. If she heard anything about the squirrel or the neighbor, she would break into tears. The loss of her favorite squirrel followed her for decades afterward. Even when she was grown, the thought or mention of that little squirrel brought tears to her eyes.

Mom Swims

Each year when I was a youngster growing up, our family took a summer vacation somewhere for a week or two. One year we drove to southern Missouri and found a scenic campground at Forsyth near a river and lakes. We liked that place so much that we returned the next several summers.

We got to know that area of southern Missouri well and learned about a swimming hole out in the boondocks. We went there several times to swim and fish. The road getting there was rough and slow.

One trip to that swimming hole proved memorable. I wish I had a video of what happened. All of us Willis kids could swim and we were playing and swimming in a pool of water in the middle of a clear running stream. The pool wasn't large, maybe six feet deep. Dad was sitting on the shore and mom waded into the water to practice her side stroke. She couldn't swim but she was trying to learn. She began gliding along in the water and then realized the water was over her head. She panicked. She tried standing up and that sent her down. When her head bobbed back up, she was flailing her arms and crying out for help, "Warren, Warren, help me, help me." Spitting water and thrashing around, she kept calling for dad to come help her.

All of us kids were close by, and seeing mom splashing up and down in that small pool of water looked so funny to us.

We started laughing hysterically, saying "Warren, Warren." Dad was sitting on the shore watching this. He shook his head, stood up, waded into the water and pulled her out. We kids kept on laughing, saying "Warren, Warren."

When we all got back to camp that evening and for several days thereafter, we kids continued to laugh and say "Warren, Warren." Mom was so embarrassed about what had happened that she walked around with her head lowered in shame. All of her young kids could splash and play in that waterhole but she had panicked in six feet of water.

When we got back home from that vacation trip, mom went straight to the YMCA for swim lessons. It wasn't long before she was swimming in deep water, and it didn't stop there. She continued her swimming at the YMCA on a regular weekly schedule, and within a few months she was swimming long distances. In fact, she became the champion long-distance swimmer in our family. She could swim 50-100 laps in the YMCA swimming pool with no problem. She was enjoying swimming and getting good exercise. Never again would anybody laugh at her in a swimming pool.

Family Games, Sports, and Activities

The Warren Willis family counted one daughter and four sons, Janet, Keith, Dale, Dean, and Wayne, until a younger daughter, Angela, was added by adoption. As youngsters, we had family fun playing board games like Monopoly. When our Grandma Jensen visited, we enjoyed playing the game of Carom with her. Grandma was the best Carom shooter.

As we grew a little older, we all branched into different sports and activities. Swimming we all did. After mom learned how to swim, she and dad and Dean became the best swimmers in the family. Dean was on the high school swim team and specialized in breast stroke. In high school and college, Dale did some springboard diving. Water skiing happened for us because we had a boat on Lake Ponderosa in Iowa. Dale, Dean, and Wayne were the best water skiers. Wayne and Dale became good snow skiers as well.

Baseball was a neighborhood sport because our high school in Marshalltown, Iowa, didn't have a baseball team. My brothers and I didn't play football or run track in high school, and I was the only one who played basketball. I was a second-stringer on the high school basketball team. Wayne was a good tumbler so he was key to the high school gymnastics team.

Our big house in Marshalltown had a basement where Wayne practiced guitar with his music band for a couple of years. We added a ping pong table to that basement which got some use. Wayne was the best but we were all competitive at ping pong.

Card games became a group activity in our home when we reached high school age. Mom and dad played lots of Bridge (card game) with their friends. We kids played a variety of card games with family and friends.

Sister Angela became a good roller skater in junior high school so she spent time hanging out at the roller rink. In junior high I took up golf and within a few years my brothers and dad were playing. Dale eventually became the better golfer.

Fishing and hunting were part of growing up in the Willis household. I did some fishing during my travel years and Dean's family took lots of fishing trips. Motorcycles were brought into the family by Dale and before long, all the Willis boys and dad owned motorcycles. Wayne won a hill-climb competition. Dale, dad, and Wayne were the better motorcycle handlers. In his later years, Dale began taking vacations with his wife on motorcycles, and Wayne is now doing the same.

Before he got married, Dale spent a summer in Hawaii and did a lot of snorkeling along the coastline. I did some snorkeling in Florida's coastal waters and Wayne is now doing some ocean swimming during vacations. When Dale lived in California near Lake Elsinore, he took up sky diving. He made lots of jumps, earned quite a few jump patches, and saw some friends get killed. Later when Dale was working and raising a family in Utah, he joined a rocket club and built his own (small) rockets. Dale's latest activity is bicycling. He's given up snow skiing due to his age but still has golf and bicycling.

During my travel years, I stopped to see brother Wayne in Colorado and he showed me a board game that he put together. It was named Capitol Hill, with a focus on political voting and major industries. We played it with friends and it was a fun game with potential. I took it with me and sent it to a promoter friend I knew in Iowa. He played the game and offered some suggestions. I made some changes to the game and typed up the rules, then submitted a written patent application that was accepted. Wayne and I paid several hundred dollars for a game patent and I sent the game back to my promoter friend in Iowa. He knew some game players who tested new board games but we didn't get a contract offer.

Youth Stories

I still have distant memories of things that happened when I was little. I was about four years old when I walked with my older sister to a country school outside Marshalltown, Iowa. There were perhaps twenty kids in that country school, and at a Christmas party there, I was coaxed into singing a Christmas song by myself. Mom and dad were happy but I was scared. Months later our family moved to the city and my mom walked me to my first day of school. One day an older man came to our house and offered to sharpen knives for some food. Mom paid him a few dollars and made him a sandwich after he sharpened her knives. While he sat on the front steps eating his sandwich, I sat down beside him and told him I wanted to be just like him someday. That made him laugh. Some older boys down the street from where we lived played a trick on me. They lit a match and told me I could put out the flame by pinching it. I did it and burned my fingers while they were laughing. The kitchen table that our family ate meals on had drawers. Sometimes during our meals I put my peas and carrots in the drawers so I wouldn't have to eat them.

The next house that we moved to was on the edge of town, near a creek and cornfield. In our basement was a plastic clothes line which I hung on one day. The line broke and I fell backward, hitting my head on the concrete floor. My memory and brain didn't work right for several weeks after that but I didn't tell anybody. No doubt I suffered a concussion. One day I took a water squirt bottle and squirted water into an electrical outlet on the outside of our house. I got a jolt of electricity and thought I broke something. I caught a gopher snake and kept it as a pet for a while. Stray cats roamed the area so our family took in stray cats for house pets. To catch small ground squirrels and gophers in our yard, my brothers and I would put on gloves and fill the ground holes with water. When the grinnies and gophers came up for air, we would grab them. My dad drove me to school one day when I was about six years old. He let me out of the car and I dashed across the street to school without looking for traffic. A car had to slam on the brakes to keep from hitting me. Dad talked to me about that after he came home from work. Our family got our first television set when I was about nine years old. That was exciting.

   We lived in two different houses by the cornfield, and then we moved to a big white house in the center of Marshalltown. Mom and dad went out one evening and a babysitter came to watch us kids. She was a nice elderly lady who lived nearby and we were acting up. She told mom and dad about our bad behavior when they got home, and the next day our parents took us to her house to apologize. I was home one day inspecting mom's sewing machine with one of my brothers, and we managed to run a needle through my finger. That hurt.

Bow and Arrow

Our family grew up in Marshalltown, Iowa. We lived in a big white house with a large backyard. The front yard was smaller. I was about twelve years old playing with a bow and arrow in the front yard one day. I don't recall who owned the bow, maybe me, but I know the arrow was solid and fitted with a sharp metal tip.

I was probably shooting at a bird in a tree when I let fly an arrow almost straight up. I missed the target and watched the arrow go up and up and up because I had pulled hard on the string. When the arrow peaked, very high, I glanced at where I thought the arrow would land. To my fright, in the front yard of a house at the end of the block were two small kids playing, maybe five and eight years old. I looked back at the arrow, which was now dropping toward the ground. Where would it land? I looked again at the spot where I thought it would come down and the kids were right there, in the target zone.

My feelings of fright rose to horror. If either of those kids got hit by that arrow, think of the consequences. Flashing through my mind were multiple bad endings to this story.

Within a few seconds the arrow landed right where I thought it would. It stuck in the ground maybe 10-20 feet from where those two kids were playing. My horror instantly lifted to huge relief. The kids were safe; I didn't kill or injure them.

Sixty years later I can still vividly remember my swing of emotions from fright to relief throughout that incident. I ran down the sidewalk to that house, grabbed the arrow sticking in the front yard, and ran back home. I'm not sure those kids even saw me retrieve the arrow. From then on, I was more observant about what direction I shot an arrow and a gun.

Scoop the Loop

I graduated from high school in 1967, and I can still remember scooping the loop during my high school years. All high schoolers in Marshalltown, Iowa, did it. In the evenings we would drive or ride in cars back and forth across town on main street, honking and waving at others scooping the loop. From main street we would turn and drive to a Dairy Queen, maybe stop there and chat with friends, then turn around and drive back to main street. We might spend twenty minutes scooping the loop or maybe a couple of hours.

Sounds pretty silly but that was our way of socializing back then. To be popular in school, you needed to be seen around town with friends. Only a small percentage of high schoolers owned cars so they were popular. They could scoop the loop with friends whenever they wanted, and also take girls out on dates. Most of the main street scooping was done in parent's cars.

My youngest brother, Wayne, was good at electronics so he rigged up a strobe signal device for scooping the loop. He could aim his strobe signal at the red traffic lights and make them turn green, like emergency vehicles do. When he and his friends scooped the loop, they didn't have to stop for as many red lights.

I've talked to other people my age who told me they scooped the loop in their hometown when they were young. Some called it "dragging the main". Everybody in high school wanted to get noticed so they drove back and forth on main street in the evenings, waving and honking at friends.

After high school, next came college or a job. College students and people working for a living had more important things to do than scooping main street after dark in cars.

Prison Break

I knew Craig from my high school years in Marshalltown, Iowa. He was an avid hunter who liked guns. He enlisted in the Army during the Vietnam War and did ground combat there. He also did military police duty.

A military prison here in the United States is where Craig served as a prison guard, and one of the inmates in that prison was a friend of Craig's. I don't recall why Craig's friend was incarcerated, but the fellow didn't like prison life and wanted to escape. He needed Craig's help. He also needed help from his girlfriend who lived in the area.

Craig went along with the plan. The inmate placed himself beside a certain door at a certain time. Craig was in the prison control room where the lockdown switches were. Craig unlocked one specific door for a matter of seconds, maybe a minute, allowing his friend to open the door. Then Craig relocked that door. The prisoner went outside and met his girlfriend who was waiting in a car.

Craig told me never to use his name if I ever talked about this story because he could be court marshaled for what he did. To my knowledge the prisoner was never caught. From what I've heard, the military doesn't search very long or very hard for AWOL soldiers.

Danger: Gasoline

I've experienced several close encounters with propane explosions over the years. Several times it happened in my motorhome, when I turned my propane stove on and the spark I gave didn't light quickly enough. When the spark came, propane in the air went "boom".

Gasoline can be just as deadly, and two instances I still remember. I was maybe twelve years old living in Marshalltown, Iowa, and decided to clean my bicycle. It was cold weather in the Fall so I took my bike down the back stairs of our house to a crude basement room. I had with me a rag and a small bucket with half an inch of gasoline in it. I began wiping and cleaning my bicycle with a gas rag.

Just a few feet away from me was the house furnace in full heat mode. I began to smell gas fumes around me and then my father walked in the back door of the house. He stopped and asked what that smell was and walked down the steps to see me cleaning my bike with gasoline.

With a shout he said, "Stop, get everything out of there!" I hustled my bike and bucket with gas to the backyard. Dad opened the two back doors to the house and fanned them to push some air into the basement. Then he looked at me and shook his head like I was the stupidest kid on Earth. And that's exactly how I felt then. How could I have been so stupid? Stupid me.

Another gasoline experience could have ended badly for me as well. I was at our Ponderosa Lake house in Montezuma, Iowa. Several people there were cleaning and raking debris in our front yard. Somebody lit a match to burn the pile of leaves and sticks but the flames weren't doing well. There was a gas can with a pour spout in a shed nearby, so I got it, intending to toss some gasoline onto the struggling flames. I was about to swing the gas can toward the fire and pitch some gasoline through the air when my dad's business partner yelled "Don't do that"! He told me flames from the fire could reach through the airborne gasoline to the can I was holding. I stopped and realized he was right. I didn't toss the gas toward the brush pile after all.

It was good advice given in the nick of time. If flames from that brush fire had traveled airborne and reached me and the gas can I was holding, it could have been bad news for me. Dad's business partner felt embarrassed about yelling at me to stop, but I felt more embarrassed for not realizing what I was about to do.

Road Hunting

As teenagers growing up in Iowa, the Willis boys went on frequent hunting excursions. Our family owned several shotguns and rifles so we hunted for rabbits, squirrels, pheasants, pigeons, even frogs.

One hunting trip had me driving the car, brother Dale in the passenger seat, and brother Dean and his friend in the back seat. Outside of town we took a dirt road in a direction we'd been before. I was driving dad's company station wagon and going at a modest speed toward a railroad crossing marked only with a warning sign. Before I reached the crossing, a train going high-speed suddenly barreled across the road. I slammed on the brakes and the car slid on dirt and gravel to within twenty feet of the tracks. That was a close call I'll never forget. If that train had T-boned our car, none of us would have survived.

After that scare we continued along the road, keeping a lookout for squirrels. When we got to a familiar large wooden bridge, I stopped the car and we all got out with shotguns. One of us went under the bridge to scare out any pigeons down there. Several flew out and we blasted away. None of us were good shots so we probably didn't hit any. When all the pigeons were flushed, we got back in the car and drove on. About a quarter mile up the road was a house and the owner came out in his front yard when we drove by. He had a pen and paper in his hand and showed us that he was writing down our license number. Maybe he would call the cops. We waved at him as we passed by, not too worried.

There were a couple of smaller bridges further up the road that we stopped at, trying for pigeons. After that, we turned around and headed back the way we came. We passed the man's house again but didn't see him. At the large wooden bridge, we stopped again to flush out any pigeons that may have returned. Again, we probably didn't hit any. Then we headed toward home by way of dirt roads, keeping an eye out for squirrels.

When we got home, I told mom about the near accident with the train. She could only shake her head. A week later I told dad the story and he said he'd had a similar incident recently. He and his work crew had been driving country roads on a job and somebody in the car said they heard a whistle. The driver slowed down while everybody looked around and suddenly a train roared across some tracks not far in front of their car. It could have been bad, so dad had a scary story of his own to tell me.

Construction Work

After college I worked for three years doing road construction and asphalt paving to pay off a student loan. The job was in my hometown in Iowa.

Several incidents I still remember from that job. One of the company's asphalt crews paved a road in a small neighboring farm town. A homeowner along that road asked the crew foreman if he would pave his driveway for $300. The foreman said yes and put the money in his pocket. The owner of the construction company drove through the small town to check on the job and saw the blacktop driveway. He went back to the home office and checked the paperwork. There was nothing in the road contract about a driveway being paved, so he got on the radio and told the crew foreman to get his ass back to the office right now. Rather than firing the foreman, the company owner cut the foreman's year-end bonus by several thousand dollars.

Another incident involved a foreman and the wife of one of his crew workers. The foreman would leave the job for a while, go visit the worker's wife, and then return to the job. The first to learn about this was the worker, from his neighbors. The news filtered up to the owner of the company who fired the guilty foreman.

A third incident was a close call for me and one I won't forget. The blacktop crew I worked on began moving equipment off a finished job. I was intending to drive a large rubber roller up a shoulder incline onto a paved road. I started driving the roller at an angle to the road and one of my coworkers came running toward me waving his arms. I stopped. He told me to drive the roller slowly up the gentle incline at a 90-degree angle to the road or the roller would tip over. I realized he was right. The big roller was tall and heavy and therefore top heavy. So I did what he suggested; I drove the roller straight at the road up the gentle slope and onto the pavement. No problem. If I had tried to drive that roller up the incline at an angle, it may have rolled because of being top heavy. I would likely have fallen off in the direction of the roll and been flattened like a pancake.

Hitchhiking

Hitchhikers are rarely seen anymore along roadways, but back in the 1960s and 1970s it was common. Oftentimes I hitchhiked from one town to another during my high school and college years.

There were some hitchhiking dos and don'ts. Always start from a busy location where traffic is going slow, preferably an on-ramp. Know your line of travel and where the cities are. Carry a map if needed. Always ask the driver if he/she is going at least as far as the next busy stop. If not, turn the ride offer down. Wait for a driver who is going to the next-good-stop location. The worst thing for a hitchhiker is being let out in the middle of nowhere with little traffic going by.

One hitchhiking trip that I took from my hometown in Iowa to southern Missouri and back lasted a week. I took one backpack and tried to locate a girl I'd met on vacation. I wasn't able to find her. On my way back I visited relatives. One of my nights during that trip I spent in jail. I went into a police station and asked if I could sleep the night in a jail cell. They said yes but not with my belt. The next morning they returned my belt when I left.

Occasionally I picked up hitchhikers when I was driving during those years, but I was always cautious about who I offered a ride to. After college my hitchhiking days ended.

Motorcycle Family

Our family grew up in Marshalltown, Iowa. My brother, Dale, was the first to get a motorcycle and dad didn't approve. Dad told Dale he couldn't have a motorcycle because they were dangerous. Dale was a young teen then and he pressed the issue to the point of buying a motorcycle anyway.

Within a couple of years, all of the Warren Willis boys had motorcycles. Dad could only sit by and watch. Our motorcycles weren't big and fast; they were dirt bikes and small street motorcycles. But motorcycles became part of the Willis family during high school and college years.

Sometimes we went dirt biking or hill climbing with friends. Dad's opinion about motorcycles gradually changed. He shopped around and bought a Harley Davidson motorcycle for himself, so he became a biker, too. The Harley that dad bought was big; it weighed something like 750 pounds. Some of my brothers rode it but I never did. On the highway dad's Harley was a fast, comfortable road machine so he took it on some distant trips.

When brother Dale was married, he did some vacationing with his wife on a motorcycle. Brother Wayne is now doing the same with his wife since his retirement.

Only one of our family has had a motorcycle accident. I spent a summer in Los Angeles during my college years and took my motorcycle along for transportation. I was riding it on a freeway and leaned right to take an off ramp. A faster car pulled along my right-hand side, forcing me to stay left. When I looked up, there was a road curb in front of me. My front wheel hit the curb at 45 mph and was damaged. The bike went down and I slid a long distance on pavement. I was fortunate to be wearing a thick jacket and helmet that day. My helmet had deep scars on the side of it.

I was taken to a hospital and released the next morning. I was off work for several days with a dislocated shoulder. My arm was in a sling for two weeks. My damaged motorcycle I had shipped back to Iowa and repaired there with insurance money.

Wayne's Band

My brother, Wayne, and his friends formed a music band when he was in sixth grade. I remember them practicing songs in our basement. There were three members in the band; Wayne played guitar and sang. They were trying hard and slowly getting better.

I was in high school then and I sponsored some dances around town with a friend of mine named John. Two dances that we scheduled included Wayne's band. John and I booked the "Shadows of Knight" at the Marshalltown  Coliseum which cost a sizeable sum of money. The "Shadows of Knight" recorded the hit song "Gloria" and were a popular rock group back then. John and I needed a cheap front band for that gig so we talked Wayne's group into playing the first half hour. On dance day Wayne's group were nervous because this was their first time in front of an audience, but they did okay. They filled the time slot and the "Shadows of Knight" played until midnight. I don't think we paid Wayne's band anything.

Another dance that John and I scheduled also included Wayne's band. We booked an out-of-town band named "Captain Beefheart and the Shipwrecks" into the local armory for a dance. We needed a front band so Wayne's group played the first thirty minutes. Then "Captain Beefheart" played the rest of the show. Wayne's band did okay. If they got paid anything, it wasn't much.

After that armory dance, I don't remember much about Wayne's band. That may have been the finale for his music group.

Rappeling With Wayne

My youngest brother, Wayne, was a good athlete in high school and did well on the school gymnastics team. He and several of his friends took up rock climbing and rope rappeling during his college years. One weekend he took all of his brothers on a rope-rappeling adventure to Ledges State Park in Iowa. It was a first for the three brothers.

At the start of that trip, I was afraid of heights. We found a rock drop-off about forty feet high where we attached a rope and swivel to a tree at the top. Then I put on a waist harness and began a slow descent down the drop-off with a rope and clamp in hand. My brothers and I took turns rappeling down the rock ledge, and each descent got a little easier and faster. By the end of that afternoon, all of us were comfortable with the height and scaling down the rocky wall. My fear of heights diminished greatly after that experience.

Five years later I was traveling around the United States in a motorhome. I needed money so I asked about a job with a crew painting water towers. I took that job only because I knew I could climb water towers without being scared out of my wits. I no longer held a fear of heights. I worked that job for several months, saved some money, and then moved on.

Shootout In CA

Brother Wayne took several trips to California during his college years, to visit brother Dale in San Bernardino. On his first trip there, the two were sitting in Dale's apartment patio, catching up on yesteryear stories. Dale's neighbor, Bob, came over and joined them for a few minutes, then left and went downstairs.

Next, Dale and Wayne heard glass breaking in the apartment beneath them so they headed downstairs to investigate. Bob and another neighbor were fighting, so Dale and Wayne did their best to separate the two. Then a wife intervened and the fight got started again. Bob grabbed a rifle in his apartment, pointed it at the neighbor, and pulled the trigger. Brother Dale was standing behind the neighbor and would have taken a bullet, but the gun didn't fire. It was loaded, but no shell in the chamber.

The neighbor rushed Bob holding the rifle, took the gun away from him, and started beating Bob with the rifle butt. Dale managed to wrestle the gun away from the pair who continued fighting until the cops showed up. Bob was hauled off to jail.

On another trip to California several years later, Wayne and my parents were visiting brother Dale for his college graduation. Wayne smoked cigarettes then, so he stepped out of Dale's apartment to go buy cigarettes. He walked to a liquor store nearby and went inside. Before walking to the counter, he stopped and checked his wallet to see if he had enough money. Just then two men opened the door behind him and pulled ski masks over their faces. Seeing this, the store owner grabbed his pistol under the counter and fired a shot at the wall near the door. The two would-be robbers turned and fled.

My brother, holding his wallet in his hands, froze and didn't move. Slowly he looked up to see the store owner holding a pistol pointed in his direction. After maybe a minute, the owner set the pistol down on the counter and apologized for the gunfire and the noise.

Wayne never saw the two robbers behind him. They left the scene lickety-split. His ears were ringing from the blast of the gunshot. He bought a pack of cigarettes and then left. A police helicopter showed up overhead as he walked out of the liquor store. They were looking for the would-be robbers.

Doppelganger

I've seen two doppelgangers in my lifetime. Once while fueling my motorhome in the San Francisco area, I saw a fellow fueling his car who looked familiar. He looked just like a friend I knew from high school and college. He was the same age and height, same face and hair, even the same mustache. I told him he was a lookalike and asked to see his driver's license. He got a kick out of showing me his CA license with his name and photo. He told me everybody has a double somewhere.

Another doppelganger turned up in the campground at Eastman Lake, CA, where I was working. I was doing ranger duty and saw a camper who looked like my dad. He wasn't an exact copy but very close. His body frame and age were similar, and his face and hair were very similar. I stopped and talked with him. He camped at Eastman Lake a number of times that summer and whenever I saw him, I stopped to say hi. He had fun with the idea of being a mirror image of my father.

Dad Retires

My dad retired from his civil engineering business in Marshalltown, Iowa, in the middle 1970s. He was reading up on experimental airplanes because he'd been a pilot in World War 2. The Experimental Aircraft Association has a fly-in convention each year at Oshkosh, Wisconsin, and dad wanted to go. I had just purchased a used motorhome so dad and I and brother Wayne took my RV to Oshkosh. It was a cheap trip.

We stayed several days at the fly-in. Dad scouted through all the different airplanes which included experimental home-builts, old historic planes, war planes, and private aircraft. There was an airshow every day. Many thousands of people were there; it was an impressive airplane rendezvous. When we got back home, dad was already planning ahead for the next EAA convention. Our whole family went to Oshkosh the following year.

In the late 1970s, my mom and dad bought a new home in central Arkansas and sold their property in Iowa. Arkansas housing was cheap then and they got a nice home near a big lake. The house wasn't large but it was very comfortable. In the backyard dad hung a birdfeeder in a tree which saw lots of activity. The big birds ruled the birdfeeder, though, so dad rigged a

bare copper wire along the tree limb holding the feeder. He would drink coffee in his kitchen chair and watch the birds at the feeder. When the big birds began chasing off the little birds, he would plug the wire into an AC outlet by his chair. The big birds would get a zap of electricity and fly off. Then dad would unplug the wire and the little birds would return and rule the feeder for a while.

My folks got into the habit of swimming in the lake each afternoon. They would walk fifty yards down to the lake and swim to an island a quarter mile offshore. The neighborhood dogs began joining them on this daily swim. Mom and dad would swim out to the island with four or five dogs paddling along behind them. They would rest on the island and then swim back to shore. A black Labrador dog from the neighborhood wanted to swim with them but he had never been around water so he didn't know how to swim. One day dad carried him into the water and helped him learn how to paddle around. After that the black Lab joined them on their daily swims to the island.

I was traveling around the country in a motorhome at the time so dad decided he and mom would do some inexpensive traveling. He bought a small trailer and fixed it up nice. Then he and mom began taking travel trips for weeks at a time. They bought gasoline and food along the way and slept at night in their trailer in parking lots. They did this for several years,

enjoying the scenery of the western United States.

From Arkansas my folk's next move was to a mobile home park in south Texas. They lived there for maybe a decade. The mobile park was big and modern with lots of activities: music, dancing, swimming, card playing, shooting pool, crafts, etc. I visited mom and dad there a number of times and enjoyed playing dominos with the seniors.

It was the late 1990s when my folks made their last move to southern Missouri. Brother Dean helped them move to Joplin where he is still living. They lived out their last years there.

Utah

I bought a used motorhome in the mid 1970s and fixed it up. Then, with a few thousand dollars in the bank, I started traveling.

That used motorhome got a workout in the coming years. I put miles on it and spent money each year for maintenance and repairs. I drove it through every continental U.S. state more than once. I took that RV across Canada. When I got a park ranger job in New Mexico, I continued living in my motorhome. I transferred to a park ranger job in California and lived in my RV there. It wasn't until I retired that I bought a small car and moved into a mobile home park in Clovis, CA. The motorhome I gave away to a friend.

Of the many states that motorhome passed through during my years of traveling, Utah was/is the most scenic. And what is more remarkable, all the scenic vistas in Utah look different and all are easy to access. My favorite is Bryce Canyon.

I saw a television documentary recently about Utah's scenery. Photographers drove into the Utah backcountry on dirt roads and took aerial videos with a flying camera. The scenery was even more beautiful than I remembered.

So if you're looking for a scenic trip, do what my brother Wayne has done. He's taken several trips across Utah on a motorcycle with his wife. They hook up a video camera on their motorcycle and let the pictures stream. When Wayne gets back home, he edits the videos, puts music to it, and emails the trip to relatives and friends.

If you don't have a motorcycle, no problem. Drive your car to and through Utah. You won't be disappointed.

Letters, Telephones, Mail, TV, Computers

Before I started my motorhome travels back in the mid 1970s, I talked to the Huss family in my hometown. They were good friends of our Willis family and they agreed to be my home mailing address. They weren't planning on leaving Marshalltown, Iowa, so I gave them access to my bank account as well. When I got on the road, I phoned them every 6-8 weeks and had them forward my mail to a city post office somewhere as general delivery. My phone calls to them were from pay phones or someone's private phone and this continued for years.

I met lots of people on the road and some of them I kept in touch with. I wrote letters in those years because computers hadn't yet arrived. I had a list of people and family that I periodically wrote letters to.

My television didn't get much use unless I was plugged into electricity somewhere, which wasn't very often. I did have a generator on my RV which I used, but my television set didn't see much activity because of my book-writing projects and lack of electric hookups.

Computers didn't enter my life until the 1990s. First they came into the workplace, so my introduction to computers began there. As the years passed, more and more of the Corps of Engineers workload happened on computers. By the time I retired, half of a park ranger's work time was spent on a computer in the office which is a sad fact. I finally purchased my own laptop computer after finishing my second published book. Since then it's been a slow learning process for me, but today I'm as dependent upon a home computer as most other people are. I still don't have a cell phone and don't plan on buying one so my home telephone is a land line.

Thunderstorm

Years ago I was on my way to the Black Hills in South Dakota. Just south of the Black Hills, I stopped my motorhome in the afternoon to eat a meal. My intention was to drive the rest of the way that evening. While eating, I saw the sky above the Hills get cloudy and then turn almost black. Lightning began to flash there so I decided to camp the night where I was.

The next day the sky was clear, so I drove to the Black Hills and found a campground with one other camper in it. That evening the sky began to darken like the previous evening. When the rain started, I went to bed. Then came thunder and lightning followed by hail the size of peas and marbles. My motorhome sounded like a war zone. Rain began streaming through the broken plastic sun covers on top of my RV. The hail lasted five to ten minutes.

Looking out my window, I could see the other camper had lights on and the same problems as me. I went outside in the rain and covered my broken sunroof covers. Then I went back to bed.

The next morning I surveyed the damage to my RV and decided to leave the area. Two nights in a row was enough warning. The thin aluminum walls of my motorhome were peppered everywhere with sizeable dents. I drove eastward to the next big city and replaced the broken sun covers on my roof. Then I located an insurance adjuster who looked at my poor RV and wrote me a check for several hundred dollars.

Now comes the more interesting part of this story. Over the next several years I lived in that motorhome and suffered through some hot summers. My RV did not have air conditioning inside it, only a fan, so when the outside summer temperature reached 100 degrees, it would be 10-15 degrees hotter inside. The hotter temperatures inside my motorhome caused an outward pressure on the walls. Gradually that heat pressure from inside pushing out against the thin aluminum walls flattened out all the dents from the hailstorm.

Two years after the hailstorm, I could walk around the outside of my motorhome and not see any hail dents at all. Even the paint showed no scarring. Amazing!

Riverboat Stories

After graduating from college, I worked road construction for three years. Then I bought a used motorhome and began traveling. To make money during my ten years of traveling around the country, I worked on riverboats that push barges up and down the Midwestern rivers. Typical work schedule on a riverboat is thirty days on the boat and thirty days off. With a dozen people working and living on a boat, I heard lots of riverboat stories during those years.

One fellow that I remember from the riverboats was Butch. He worked as a ship's Mate who supervised the deckhand laborers. Butch was a big, burly guy who was easy to work with. He usually had a big smile on his face.

Butch told me some stories about his younger years when he prowled the city streets and bars with friends. One friend that he hung out with liked to cause trouble. They were sitting at a bar table one time and his friend got half drunk and threw an ash tray at a big, beautiful wall mirror behind the bar. He got a kick out of seeing the mirror shatter into a hundred pieces.

Another time Butch and his troublemaker friend were walking along a city sidewalk. Walking toward them were two Black guys who looked like gangbangers. When they met, Butch and his friend blocked the sidewalk and told the gangbangers they would have to turn around and go back the way they came from. The two gangbangers had their hands in their jacket pockets and looked at each other. Then two gunshots rang out. Both Butch and his friend grabbed their stomachs and went running away with bullet wounds. The two Black guys just continued walking along the sidewalk in the direction they were headed.

Both Butch and his friend got stitched up in a hospital. I asked to see his bullet wound and Butch showed me a small caliber bullet scar on the side of his stomach.

A similar story came from a riverboat deckhand. One evening he went to a bar by himself and after a few drinks he was feeling tipsy. Two attractive females approached him and asked if he would like to leave the bar with them and have some fun. He followed them outside to a car where the car door opened. A big Black guy got out of the car, pointed a pistol at his stomach, and pulled the trigger. Then the Black man told him to take off his clothes. Not wanting to catch another bullet, the bleeding deckhand peeled out of his clothes down to his shorts. The pimp then told him to get lost so he ran down the street to find help. The big pimp and the two ladies gathered up the deckhand's valuables, got in their car, and drove off.

Reenactments and Television

When I worked at Fort Selden State Monument, NM, in the late 1980s, there were occasions when our ranger staff dressed up in 1880s soldier garb. Schools in the area sometimes asked for a ranger presentation about the fort and soldiers.

Every couple of months Fort Selden would have a reenactment day. Staff and volunteers would dress up like soldiers or women from the 1880s. We didn't talk the part; we spoke like people from 1990, but we looked like people from 1880. The local newspaper would advertise the event and the public would come to see the reenactors at the fort. On one occasion we invited a large reenactment group from Albuquerque, and they came for the weekend. They camped overnight on the fort grounds. Some of them were dressed as Union troops, some as Rebel troops, others were wives or camp followers.

One day we got a phone call at Fort Selden from a television film crew. They wanted to do a TV travel show about Fort Selden. They showed up in a large new motorhome, a husband and wife in their mid-thirties with a film crew. They walked through the museum and fort grounds the first day and did some video takes. That night they stayed at the fort, and the next day they asked for video clips from the Fort Selden rangers. I wore a soldier uniform and carried a long rifle. I gave a short talk to the camera about the soldiers and Indians of a hundred years ago. The fort was built in the middle of Apache country.

They wanted me to demonstrate the long rifle, so I loaded it with black powder and fired it in the air. There was a loud boom with a shower of black smoke out the end of the gun. The sound man stopped the filming and said he needed to check and see if his sound equipment had blown out. Did he get the boom or not? He listened to a review of the clip and said the gunshot came through loud and clear.

It was a few months later that I got word from my mother. She told me that one of my cousins had seen me on a television travel show. I don't remember the name of the show, and back then I hadn't heard of it, but I may have gotten a few minutes of television showtime somewhere.

Photography

I took up photography after moving to California. I was in my early forties then, working as a park ranger at Lake Kaweah. My boss liked photography so he encouraged me to use a Corps of Engineers camera to take pictures around the lake. Within a few months I had purchased my own slide camera. I took lots of pictures but only a few were quality.

My boss and his wife belonged to a local camera club so I joined. My picture-taking skills slowly improved and my pictures got better. Our camera club met every month in Visalia (city) to mingle and show slides that members had taken. There were four categories for slide competition: pictorial, nature, travel, and photojournalism. I did better in the photojournalism category because I took pictures of people doing things at the lake. Photojournalism portrays some kind of story or activity.

Our camera club also competed against other camera clubs in the central California Valley. Once a month all of the Valley camera clubs would gather together for competition. All photographers were encouraged to come. Photographers from each club would submit slides in the four different categories. A judge would view each slide on a large screen in front of an audience and give it a score for merit.

At the end of the year the different camera clubs were ranked according to member score totals. Individual photographers were ranked in each of the categories. Awards were given out for best total scores and best pictures. It was a fun hobby for everyone involved.

Lake Kaweah also had an annual photo contest, sponsored by the District Corps of Engineers. Each Corps Lake was asked to submit slide photos for different picture categories. At year's end the slides were judged and shown at an annual park ranger conference. It was fun for Corps rangers to win a photo contest category.

During this time I put together several slide shows of my own that I showed to various groups of viewers. I put together a slide show about good versus bad picture-taking. I put together a pictorial slide show and several entertaining slide shows of people.

When I transferred from Lake Kaweah to Eastman Lake in central California, I continued shooting pictures and changed camera clubs. My new Madera camera club competed in the same Central Valley slide competition that I'd been involved in at Visalia. There were some very good photographers in the Madera camera club so we were strong in competition.

By the latter 1990s I was working on a book project so my photography got set aside. Gradually I lost interest in picture-taking and gave it up. It was a fun hobby for me for a number of years, though.

Painting With Teeth

I called a carpet cleaning service in Visalia, CA, to clean the carpet in my motorhome. I was given an address in the city where the carpet cleaner would meet me. I drove to that location and parked.

While waiting at that residence, I walked the sidewalk outside and saw an open garage next door. Inside the garage I could see a man in a wheelchair painting a picture with a paintbrush in his teeth. I looked around and then looked back to see if I was really seeing what I thought I was seeing. A guy sitting in a wheelchair had a picture canvas in front of him, and he was painting on the canvas with a paintbrush in his teeth.

The cleaning man drove up and a lady came out of her house to meet him. He told her he would spend twenty minutes cleaning my carpet first, and then clean the carpet inside her home. She was fine with that. He started the rug-cleaning process in my RV and I approached the lady and asked about her neighbor. She said he was a well-known local artist and she told me his name. I recognized the name because I'd seen him on television, either in a news clip or a documentary.

I walked over to the painter and asked if I could watch. He acknowledged me and continued painting. His wife came into the garage and said hi. She did some busy work for him and then went back into the house. They were in their thirties.

Looking at his canvas, I could see how he was able to paint a picture. He didn't start from scratch. His canvas already had a nice landscape scene sketched out. Somebody else had drawn a lovely landscape showing a building and other things, using straight lines and curved lines. This painter was adding colored paint to the surface of the sketched landscape.

I knew his paintings were selling for sizeable sums of money; that I had learned from the television program. What I wondered as I watched him paint was whether his sketch artist was receiving a share of the sales money.

California Sights

I've been across much of California. It's a big state with lots to see. I'm now retired in central California so I'm not far from Yosemite, Kings Canyon, and Sequoia National Parks. Yosemite and Sequoia are prime tourist attractions. A few years ago I took a trip north to Redding and saw Lake Shasta for the first time. From there I drove to Reno, Nevada, by way of Lassen Volcanic National Park and Susanville. I've seen northern California and driven into Oregon through Redwood National Park.

I've been across the Golden Gate Bridge and visited San Francisco more than once. I took a boat ride to Alcatraz Island but didn't see any ghosts there. I took a tour through the Winchester Mystery House in San Jose but no ghosts there either. The highway 1 coastline drive took days for my old motorhome to complete; it is long and winding. The Los Angeles metro area I've driven through and that is scary, like metro New York City.

At the beginning of each year, the California Corps of Engineers District schedules a park ranger conference. Those conferences took me to places like Moro Bay, Pismo Beach, Santa Cruz, Hearst Castle, and Monterey Bay Aquarium.

My traveling days are pretty much behind me now. I'm currently focused on quiet, relaxed retirement in Clovis, CA. I've grown accustomed to California and the climate here. Winter in central California lasts only six weeks and the temperature may drop to freezing. During summer, air conditioning becomes important because it's hot for three months. But the yearly climate in central California is very livable. I can golf all year-round here. Maybe that's why there are so many people living in this state.

Bonnie and Clyde and Pretty Boy Floyd

A lady friend who I know well told me a story about her father. His parents both died when he was young which resulted in him and his sister being placed in an orphanage in Oklahoma. His sister stayed in the orphanage but he ran away at age thirteen. He grew up in Oklahoma struggling on his own. About age twenty he was detained by police and he had no identification card. He looked like Pretty Boy Floyd, the gangster who was on the loose then, so the police put him in jail until they could verify who he was. Several days later Pretty Boy Floyd was seen robbing a bank elsewhere so the cops released him from jail. After that the father joined the Dust Bowl crowd headed for California where he found work picking crops on the west coast.

Another lady I know told me a story that came from her husband. Her husband's grandfather came to America from Croatia and settled in Oklahoma. He somehow got to know some of the gangsters of the 1930s, including Pretty Boy Floyd and Bonnie and Clyde. Those criminals and others sometimes hid out for a time at the grandfather's place and he would bring them food.

Clyde Barrow and Bonnie Parker became targets of the FBI and Texas Rangers after their crime sprees in 1932/33. They killed a number of people, including some police officers. In 1934 federal agents finally tracked down relatives of a gang associate of Bonnie and Clyde. They learned that the duo would soon be returning to a small Louisiana parish. Lawmen took up hiding places along a roadway and when Clyde's car showed up, the bullets began to fly.

That bullet-ridden car in which Bonnie and Clyde died is on public display in Primm, Nevada today. I've seen it numerous times. It is in Whiskey Pete's Casino encased in plexiglass along with historic photos, mementos, and documented information. The vehicle looks shiny and swank except for the many bullet holes. Back in the day it would have been a very classy car.

Gambling Fever

Several years ago I took a lady friend to an Indian casino not far from my home in Clovis, CA. The casino had a promotion that day; every hour a hot seat would be selected at random for a $500 payoff. We made a pact that if either of us won the hot seat, the other person would receive $100 of the prize money. A couple of hours later my lady friend won the hot seat money so she gave me $100.

Recently she and I went to the same casino for an overnight gambling trip. We ate a noon meal and she didn't feel well afterward so she went to the room and laid down. After resting awhile, she felt better and headed down to the slot machines. That evening we ate a meal and afterward she didn't feel right so I suggested she go to the room. She nixed that idea because she said she was on a gambling trip and needed to work the slots.

We separated among the slot machines and I was playing a bonus game when I heard my name called over the intercom. I looked around, wondering where I was supposed to go. Maybe I had won a hot-seat prize? A blackjack dealer saw who I was and pointed toward the casino cash attendants. When my slot-machine bonus ended, I cashed out and heard my name called again over the intercom. I headed toward the casino cash attendants and told them who I was; my name had been called over the intercom. They didn't know anything about me. A security guard figured out who I was and signaled me to follow him. We went through a door into a small room and there, lying on the floor, was my friend. She was awake with three EMT medics beside her. She had gotten dizzy at the slot machines and went to the restroom where she passed out.

A paramedic showed up and took her vital signs. He recommended she go to a hospital so she agreed. I went to our room, gathered our things, and drove home. The next day she called me and said she was feeling better. Doctors at the hospital had diagnosed her with an advanced bladder infection. It took a week of strong prescription medicine to get her cured.

Near Crashes

Everyone has witnessed close calls, close encounters, near misses, near accidents in their lifetime. I'm going to replay here a couple of near accidents I've had while driving a car.

A lady friend and I were driving to Laughlin, Nevada, from central California. As we approached Laughlin on highway 163, a detour rerouted traffic along a southerly highway overlooking the city. I was driving my small Saturn car and stopped at an intersection stop sign about a mile from the detour. I could see Laughlin on my left so I started a left turn, but then came a shout! I stopped. My passenger pointed at a car coming from the opposite direction that wasn't slowing down. It was then that we both noticed there was no stop sign for oncoming traffic at that intersection. That car whizzed past me at 50 mph. Had I turned left in front of that vehicle, my car would have been T-boned on the passenger side.

Another close call came while I was driving to Las Vegas with the same lady, this time in her car. With us were her granddaughter and her young daughter and husband. Halfway to Vegas we were nearing the town of Four Corners. I was driving behind a semi-truck and I had the vehicle automatic speed control turned on. The truck slowed as we approached a two lane highway, but my speed control maintained my speed so I took the left lane, intending to pass the truck before reaching the two lane road ahead. The interstate made a gentle right curve as I was passing the truck; then came another truck from the opposite direction. We all met where three lanes merged into two lanes. Our three vehicles passed side by side on a two lane highway, with my Jeep in the middle.

Fortunately, both truckers were paying attention and saw my predicament. They both pulled their trucks to the right onto the road shoulders, giving me room in between. I was driving on the center yellow line as I sped up and passed the trucker on my right.

When I pulled my car into the single lane ahead of the semi-truck, I was safe and the crisis was over. Then came the chatter from passengers in my car about what they thought of my driving skills. All I could do was hang my head in shame.

Dollar for the Needy

On a trip to Reno, NV, I stopped at a small casino and walked past a lady sitting outside on a sidewalk. She looked poor so I gave her a dollar and went inside the casino. A few minutes later I looked up and there she was, playing the slot machines for five cents a poke.

I drove to a Fresno Grizzlies baseball game and parked my car. Walking to the stadium, I passed a homeless guy with his hand out. I opened my wallet and handed him two dollars. Then he asked for another dollar; he said he needed a little more money. I reached down, snatched the two dollars back and went to the ball game.

A homeless young man was sitting on a sidewalk in downtown Fresno, looking dirty and without shoes. I walked by him, then stopped and offered him two dollars. He looked at it and said he needed six dollars for a Subway sandwich. I held the two dollars out for him and he said he couldn't use it; he needed six dollars to eat. I put the two dollars back in my wallet and walked on.

One lady became a regular on my trips to and from a Fresno golf course. She dressed the part and always stood at the same stop light. Sometimes she had her leg wrapped with cardboard and bandages. Other times she had on dark glasses for blindness. She held a cardboard sign asking for donations. My car was stopped beside her one day at the stop light so I asked where she lived. She told me she lived just down the street. I didn't have a dollar bill so I gave her the coins in my coin purse.

Driving a Fresno freeway one day, I took an off ramp and stopped at a traffic light. Sitting by the road were two seniors, a man about seventy years old and a lady about sixty. The lady was sitting on a plastic bucket with her head down. I looked in my wallet and all I had were twenties. The two seniors looked so desperate that I took out a twenty-dollar bill and folded it. Rolling down my car window, I motioned to the guy who walked over and took the bill. He thanked me and handed it to the lady. She didn't look up; she took the bill in her hand, then glanced at the corner of it. Then she looked again at the corner of the bill and raised her head and nodded to me. That was her thanks from someone in need.

Drone Pilot

What I know about drone airplanes comes from television. TV news clips and documentaries show unmanned aircrafts capable of flying high for long periods of time. The first drones were small and fitted with video equipment. Then came the larger weaponized drones that can take pictures and shoot missiles. People flying the drones are located somewhere on the ground using sophisticated computers.

Action movies sometimes feature a person flying a remote aircraft from a desktop computer. But in real life, how often will we see, meet, or talk with a real drone pilot?

Not long ago I was golfing in Fresno, and midway through my round I joined up with two golfers ahead of me. They were brothers in their thirties; one lived in Las Vegas. The brother from Vegas said he was in the Air Force, stationed at Creech Air Force base. I asked if he was a pilot and he told me the name of a plane he flew. I didn't recognize the name of his airplane and asked if it was a rotary craft. He told me it was a drone.

Now I'm interested because this soldier is telling me he flies drone airplanes. I quizzed him further about his piloting job and the drones he flies. He couldn't share details because that information is classified, but I learned that the drones he flies can spy and shoot missiles. And his pilot training is similar to what air traffic controllers do. A drone pilot needs strong computer skills as well as a good memory, plus the ability to multi-task in pressure situations.

Suffice to say that Creech Air Force base in Las Vegas isn't far from Area 51 in Nevada which is a top-secret military zone.

Tickets

A friend and I took a trip to Florida during my college years. We drove and slept in an old van and stopped in cities along the way. Parking was never a problem for us because we paid no attention to parking signs or parking tickets. Whenever we got a parking ticket, which happened, it went in the garbage. Who would be able to catch us or find us?

In the mid 1970s I began traveling around the country in a motorhome, and the same pattern applied. If I got a ticket somewhere, who would make me pay? Nobody could find me. So when I got an occasional parking ticket, it went in the wastebasket. I didn't get many, but parking tickets were a joke. What irritated me was people and cops telling me I couldn't park my RV overnight somewhere. That happened a lot because I didn't camp overnight in campgrounds; I camped overnight in free parking areas.

One morning there was a knock on my door. A ranger at a Colorado park informed me that I was parked in a place where overnight camping wasn't allowed. He pointed to a sign that said so. I gave him my driver's license and he said he was going to have to write me a citation for the violation. As I sat waiting for him to finish, I asked him if he really thought I was going to pay the ticket. My license plates were from Iowa. He looked at me and said I had better pay it because this was a federal citation. He finished and gave me the citation and told me to move my RV. I got dressed, put the citation in the trash, and drove on.

In Oregon, I was parked by a coastal river where salmon were making a spawning run upriver. Quite a few anglers were along the shoreline. I talked to some of the fishermen and learned that it was legal to fish for salmon on one side of a bridge but not on the other side of the bridge. They told me it was a ticket trap for Fish and Game Wardens.

I got my fishing pole and looked around for game wardens because I didn't have an Oregon fishing license. I put a treble hook on my fishing line and started casting. Salmon rarely bite during a spawning run so I was trying to snag a fish rather than hook it in the mouth. I snagged a couple of Chum salmons, maybe ten pounds each, reeled them in and released them. After a couple of hours, I quit and went back to my RV.

That evening there came a knock on my door; it was a game warden. He said he had seen me fishing and wanted to check my fishing license. I told him I didn't have an Oregon fishing license and I wasn't fishing. He asked me to open a rear box on my RV and I asked if he had a warrant. He said if I didn't open the box, he would take me to jail, so I opened the box. He saw my fishing pole and said he recognized it. He took the fishing pole and wrote me a citation for fishing without a license. I could get the pole back when I paid the ticket. The pole was cheap, maybe a $20 price item. The ticket went in the wastebasket.

I was in southern Montana one summer, fishing for trout in the Yellowstone River. I had no schedule so I fished there for several months. A state Fish and Game Warden checked my fishing license one day and I didn't have one. He wrote me a ticket, and this time I paid it because I wanted to stay in that area and continue fishing. I mailed a check for the fine to the Montana Department of Fish and Game and then went to a bait shop and bought a Montana fishing license. I was checked several more times after that by Fish and Game Wardens and proudly showed them my Montana fishing license.

Tax Dollars at Work

I worked many years for a federal agency so I saw wasteful spending as part of the job. If there are ways of squandering money, the federal government has already done it. Private businesses can't operate that way; they work on profit margins. But cities, states, and federal governments carry on in spite of fiscal mismanagement.

I still remember two state waste projects from my traveling years, and by waste, I mean money. I was somewhere along the Atlantic coast in the southeast U.S., driving a road next to the ocean. On the ocean side of the road, I came upon a day-use park with concrete tables and firepits. The tables had seats and overhead roofs and there were concrete blocks around the firepits. The site was abandoned; nobody was there because of deep, loose sand. Planners had forgotten that Mother Nature can move loose sand around with winds, tides, and surf.

Another state park I visited was in Wyoming. I drove by the park and the facilities looked nice. It was free camping so I decided to stay a few days. Nobody was there. That evening I heard a noise in my motorhome so I baited a mouse trap. It wasn't long before the trap snapped. I threw the dead mouse outside and after a while came more noises. I baited a couple of more traps and before long I had another dead mouse.

I went to bed that night and the rustling of mice went on all night. I got up time and again to bait traps and toss dead mice outside. In the morning it was time to leave. I knew why there were no people in this park. It was ruled by field mice; they were everywhere. Somebody at state management level had come up with the idea of building a state park at this location. What they forgot to check first was statistics on field mice in the area. It was a shame that this modern state park wasn't usable because of mice.

Windy Coast

Years ago I drove through Olympic National Park. The Olympic Peninsula, just west of Seattle, is plush and scenic. From there I headed my motorhome south along the Washington state coast. It was Fall season so there was plenty of wind and rain happening. That coastal drive had my RV swaying side to side from the ocean winds. There were some days that I didn't drive because of strong winds. When I reached Oregon, it was more of the same: wind and rain.

Somewhere along that drive, either in Washington or Oregon, I stopped for the evening at a blacktopped vista overlook. The vista set atop a cliff adjacent to the ocean. The wind was blowing hard and then the rain started. A police car pulled in alongside my RV. Despite the wind and rain, the officer got out of his car and knocked on my door. I was sure he was going to tell me I couldn't park there for the night so I opened the door and told him I wasn't leaving. I wasn't going to move my RV at that late hour in the dark. He told me he was offering me a warning. Sometimes the wind from the ocean blows so strong up that cliff face that vehicles can be overturned. I told him I would be leaving the vista immediately. He was soaking wet when he got back in his squad car.

I navigated my motorhome carefully back onto the roadway. Through the wind and rain, I drove maybe five miles inland to a small town where I parked for the night. Surprise, surprise, the wind velocity dropped by 50% after driving just a few miles inland.

I learned some things about winds and climate in the Northwest U.S. on that trip. Winds along the Washington and Oregon coastlines, especially during Fall and Spring seasons, can be strong. But inland the winds diminish or subside. As for rainfall, expect that for six months each year in both states.

Northern California is a different story. I drove the California coast highway from north to south, and wind from the ocean was no problem. Northern California has mild climate without strong winds or heavy rainfall. Rugged terrain in northern California is why there aren't many roads or people living there.

Cowgirl

In the mid 1990s my job took me to Eastman Lake in central California. That park is surrounded by cattle range, and occasionally I talked to the neighboring cattle ranchers. One of those ranchers passed away and he willed his grazing land and cattle to a relative living in a nearby city. She was a nice lady, about thirty-five years old. I met her when she came to the lake to inspect her cattle herd and property. I talked with her from time to time and she told me an interesting story.

She had a city job when she inherited the cattle and land from her relative. Shortly after the inheritance was completed, she got a visit from a taxman. He wanted a sizeable inheritance tax for the State of California. She told him she didn't have any money, certainly not the tens of thousands of dollars that the State wanted. So they sat down and arranged an annual payment plan to pay off her inheritance tax.

Several months later the lady decided to change her lifestyle. She quit her job, sold some cattle, and then purchased a large canvas tent, a portable generator, and a quad runner. She moved onto her grazing land and brought a partner with her. The two ladies lived in the big canvas tent, tending cattle. I sometimes saw them riding around on the quad runner.

Maybe a year later the two ladies and the cattle disappeared from that property. I asked about them and learned that the lady had moved back to town. Living in a tent in the middle of pastureland wasn't an easy life, and she wasn't getting rich raising cows. So she sold her cattle and went back to city life.

Animal Stories

I still remember some animal stories from my time at Eastman Lake in California. One morning I was driving through the day-use side of the lake and standing in front of the restroom at the beach area was a full-grown wild turkey, five feet tall. When I stopped my truck and rolled down the window, the turkey began cackling and flapping its wings at me, like it was looking for a mate. It hung around that area for a couple of days before wandering off.

We held a fishing tourney for kids one year with lots of activities, prizes, and free meals for participants. One of our volunteers dressed up in a Bobby Beaver suit and walked around to promote water safety. She got hot inside the suit so she went into a restroom to take it off. A little girl in the restroom came running out, saying "Mommy, mommy, there's a bear in the bathroom."

One of our campground hosts bought a new video recorder. He assembled it in his motorhome at the campground and then saw a lynx through his front windshield. It was a beautiful full-grown lynx standing across a road by a restroom. He started filming as the lynx looked side to side and then started walking toward his motorhome. His little dog was tied up outside and started barking. Hearing his dog bark, the camp host realized why the lynx was interested in his campsite. He quickly put down his video camera and ran outside to rescue his little dog. The lynx ran away.

Another volunteer staying in the campground told me a funny story. He was bicycling around the campground for exercise one day and saw three deer running together along the edge of the campground. A single coyote was chasing them. He stopped cycling and watched to see what would happen. The animals disappeared behind a restroom. When they reappeared around the other side of the restroom, the lone coyote was being chased by the three deer.

This next story dates back to my high school years. Our family was at our Ponderosa Lake house in Iowa where we were boating and fishing. My brother, Dean, somehow caught a live mouse and showed it around. To see what would happen, he walked out on the dock and tossed the mouse into the water. The mouse didn't sink; it bobbed around and paddled its feet. Suddenly there was a swirl in the water and the mouse disappeared. A bass sucked it up. My brother talked about that for days afterward because he was a fisherman. If he had tied a fish line and hook to that mouse, he would have caught a nice bass. It was a missed opportunity.

I'm now living in Clovis, CA, not far from a golf course where I play golf. The tree squirrels there see lots of golfers so they aren't afraid of people. Some of the golfers feed the squirrels. One day I finished my round of golf and was standing beside the last green. A squirrel walked up to me and sat down on my toe. He wanted food. He sat there with paws raised, looking up at me, waiting. I felt bad for him because I didn't have any food to offer. When I got home, I wrote down on my grocery list: buy peanuts at the Dollar store. Now I carry peanuts with me on the golf course.

Bicycle Traveler

I was driving a park ranger pickup from Eastman Lake to Madera, CA, one afternoon. Halfway there I saw a fellow walking his bicycle along the roadway. I stopped and asked if he had trouble. Both tires on his bicycle were flat so I told him to toss his bike in the back of my pickup. I would give him a lift to town which was five miles away.

I don't remember seeing a backpack; he may have had a small pack on his back. He sat down in the passenger seat and looked like a homeless guy, about forty-five years old. What made him unusual was his big smile. He was very cheerful and happy to get a ride.

I quizzed him about where he was headed and he told me he was headed to Baker, CA, where he had a place to stay. I don't recall if he said where he was coming from or how long he'd been traveling, but he smelled so bad that he obviously hadn't bathed for a long time. It didn't look like he owned much more than the clothes he was wearing, but he was cheerfully confident about making it to Baker with his bicycle, 200 miles away. He didn't lose his smile as he told me his story.

At the edge of town I pulled into a gas station and told the fellow this was as far as I was going. I gave him a few dollars and he pulled his bike out of the back of my truck. As he began walking away, he smiled and waved and thanked me again.

Watching him pushing his bicycle, I was still struck by his big smile. Here was a guy who had nothing but the clothes on his back, and a bicycle with two flat tires, walking toward a city 200 miles away. And yet he was still smiling and cheerful. How many people in the world in that situation would be smiling?

Two Boats

It was late Fall at Eastman Lake and the weather was cold and windy. Only two boaters showed up to try their luck fishing.

Boater 1 launched his boat and fished along the campground side of the lake. Then he headed toward the upper end of the lake. Across the water, Boater 2 launched his boat and headed directly for the upper end of the lake. Boater 1 was bundled up in the cold air, driving his boat and looking around. Boater 2 was bundled up with a scarf wrapped around his face, looking forward. He wasn't looking around and didn't see Boat 1.

As the two boats got closer, Boater 1 assumed the other boater could see him. But Boat 2 continued on a path aimed in front of Boat 1. When Boater 1 finally realized that Boater 2 wasn't paying attention, it was too late. The two boats collided. Both boats were damaged but neither took on water.

I heard about this accident from Boater 1 a week later. Boating accidents occasionally happen on lakes, but this one was memorable. Only two boats were operating on the lake that day during daylight hours, and they managed to run into each other.

Jail Time

When I worked at Eastman Lake in CA, I met a lot of boaters and fishermen. One fisherman that I became acquainted with was a nice guy; I saw him every week or two at the dock. He told me one day that he wouldn't be seeing me again for awhile. I asked why not and he said he was going to jail. That surprised me so I asked for the story.

He said he and a business partner owned a gun store in a nearby city, and his partner made some illegal gun sales. The cops found out and arrested both owners of the business. The two owners were charged with crimes and the gun shop was closed. The fisherman told me he wasn't aware of his business partner's illegal dealings but he was equally liable for the crimes. The police wanted information about the buyers of the guns so the partner offered a plea deal. He would give testimony about the illegal gun sales in return for a reduced jail sentence. The police and lawyers agreed.

So the partner gave full testimony, and both gun shop owners were found guilty of illegal gun sales. They both received four years in prison. But because the police needed the partner's testimony about who the guns were sold to, the partner's sentence was cut in half. He got two years.

A Fish Tale

I tried to keep abreast of how the fish were biting when I worked at Eastman Lake in CA. I talked to fishermen about which fish were biting, where, how deep, etc. Eventually I began emailing a weekly Eastman Lake fish report to a local newspaper. Sometimes I included a "fisherman of the week" if somebody caught a big fish. The newspaper put the fishing information in its sports section.

One evening I was patrolling the Eastman docks. A fisherman I knew brought his boat in and he showed me a 10-pound bass he'd caught. It was a beauty. He said he didn't feel like cleaning the fish, could I give it away to somebody who would want it? I told him I would try so he gave the big fish to me and departed.

A few minutes later another boat motored to the dock; it was a young man I'd seen a few times. I asked how he did and he said he didn't catch many fish. I asked if he wanted a 10-pound bass; would he take it home and make use of it if I gave it to him? He said "yes", so I gave him the big bass.

About a week later I talked to a senior fisherman at the boat dock. I asked if the fish were biting. He hadn't done well that day but he said a young fellow he knew caught a big fish at Eastman a week earlier. I was curious and asked for details. He said he saw the fish; it was a 10-pound bass. I asked what the young man looked like and how old he was? The old fisherman described the young fisherman I'd given the 10-pound bass to.

So I broke the bubble and told the guy that the bass he'd seen a week earlier came from me. A fisherman I knew caught the fish and gave it to me, then I gave it to the young man. The senior fisherman began to chuckle as this fish story stretched out. He said he needed to have another chat with the young fisherman about his big catch.

Get the Facts

During my years working as a park ranger in California, I saw lots of comical things. Some of those funnies came from my supervisors.

One afternoon while patrolling Eastman Lake, I took notice of a powerful white ski boat pulling two skiers around the lake. Later that afternoon at the day-use dock, a young man approached me. He pointed toward deep water, where two ski rope handles were bobbing on the surface of the water, and said his boat had capsized. The driver had turned too sharp and a wave washed over the boat. There were no injuries. I wrote down his information and he said his family would come to the lake the following day and retrieve the boat.

At the office I wrote an incident report and put it on the manager's desk. The next morning at headquarters the senior ranger was discussing the sunk boat with the manager. I drove to the day-use area and the family members were already there, in the process of retrieving their sunk boat. They had another boat on the water slowly pulling the ski ropes attached to the sunk boat. The father had a truck parked at the dock with a long cable winch. He told me he would pull the boat onto a trailer when it was close enough.

I left there and patrolled the other side of the lake, then returned to the office. The park manager was on the telephone with his District boss, talking about the sunk boat. An hour later I drove back to the day-use dock to check on the boat recovery, and everybody was gone. The sunk boat had been trailered, drained of water, and driven away.

When I returned to headquarters, the park manager emerged from his office and made an announcement to the Eastman staff. A decision had been made about the sunk boat. He and his boss in District had decided there would be no recovery allowed for the sunk boat until a written safety plan had been drawn up by the boat owner. The safety plan needed to be presented to the Eastman manager and approved before recovery of the boat could commence. The reason for this was the danger of diving in deep water. The boat recovery plan would have to minimize the danger of diving in sixty feet of water. This paperwork could require a few days for the owner to complete so the boat may not be raised for a week or so.

When he finished his speech, I told him the sunk boat was already gone. He asked how that was possible and I told him the owner pulled it to shore using ski ropes. The manager scratched his head, returned to his office, and called his District boss. His half day of planning and phone calls had been for naught.

This incident is a classic example of government operation versus private enterprise. Government operation requires layers of paperwork whereas private enterprise can move quickly.

Here's another Eastman Lake memory that I can still laugh about. A senior ranger from another Corps lake was assigned to fill in as temporary manager at Eastman for a couple of weeks. He wanted to show himself a capable leader. I went to work after a weekend off and put several rolls of dollar coins on my desktop. I was responsible for maintaining the entrance fee station which used dollar coins. My routine was to buy dollar coins at a bank with my money, bring them to work, and sell them to the Corps of Engineers for use in the fee machine.

After a patrol around the lake, I returned to the office to find the rolls of coins on my desk gone. I asked about the coins and the interim manager called me into his office. He began reprimanding me for leaving Corps money in the open, unsecured. His rant continued for several minutes and he said he was considering writing a disciplinary report on me. I didn't say anything; I just let him stick his foot deeper down his throat. When he finished, I went to the office secretary.

She was a nice, capable lady and when I told her who owned the dollar coins, she quickly opened the office safe and returned them to me. As I walked past the manager's office, he reminded me again about keeping the coins secure. It was then that I let him know his mistake; the dollar coins didn't belong to the Corps of Engineers. They belonged to me. He had pilfered my coins from my desk.

When the new manager heard this, he knew immediately that he'd buried himself. His first day on the job and he'd forgotten the very first rule of management: get all the facts first. He didn't have any words of explanation or excuse, nor did he apologize. We didn't hear any more from him the rest of the day.

Cross Country

An interesting thing happened one day when I was working at Fort Selden State Monument in New Mexico. Two vans showed up in the parking lot about noon and a lady came into the museum. She asked if she could set up tables in the parking lot to feed some bicycle riders. I said that was fine and followed her outside to find out what was happening. She and another lady set up several tables and began hurriedly making sandwiches and setting out food and drinks. A bicycler cruised up and stopped and began eating. Then another group of cyclists stopped and then more and more. The ladies continued making sandwiches as fast as they could.

I asked the bikers what was happening, and they told me they were on a cross-country bicycle ride. It would take them a couple of weeks to finish their journey. The top American cross-country cyclist at that time was part of the group. He was married to the lady fixing sandwiches. All the riders had paid a fee up front to join this cross-country bike ride. Food and motels along the way were part of the package deal. It was a vacation for all of them, but imagine a vacation where you bicycle several thousand miles across country. Not for me.

I gave the bikers some history about why the fort was built and offered to shoot a black-powder rifle for them. They wanted to see that so I got a long rifle and loaded it with powder. The boom got their attention. When they all finished eating, off they went down the highway toward their next destination. Needless to say, all of those twenty cyclists were physically fit. No fatties in that group.

Carbon Monoxide

It was a quiet weekend at Lake Kaweah in CA. I was the only park ranger on duty that day. Late in the morning I drove to the river below the dam and gave an interpretation talk to a group of high schoolers. Then I headed back to lake headquarters.

At the office a maintenance worker found me and told me what had happened while I was gone. He was driving through a recreation area at the upper end of the lake and passed an odd sight in the parking lot. A car was parked there with the engine running and a hose connected to the exhaust pipe. The hose stretched into the driver's side window.

The maintenance worker stopped his truck to investigate. The doors and windows of the car were locked so he shouted at the driver sitting in the driver's seat with his eyes closed. The driver opened his eyes and looked over, then shook his head "no". He wasn't going to open the door. So the worker ran to his truck and grabbed a crowbar. When he threatened to break the car window, the driver opened the door. The maintenance man pulled the exhaust hose from the car, then questioned the man to find out what condition he was in.

It turned out that the driver had just begun to gas himself, so he wasn't yet affected by the fumes. The worker stayed and talked with the guy for a short time to make sure he could drive home. Then the worker confiscated the hose and left the scene.

After hearing this story, I gave thanks to the maintenance man for being in the right place at the right time. I drove back to the recreation area and the vehicle was gone. In the days ahead I related this incident to a veteran sheriff deputy who'd seen numerous suicides during his years of duty. He described them as "a long-term solution to a short-term problem".

Pro Golf

Decades ago I went to two professional golf tournaments. The golf course was in Ohio. There were back-to-back PGA tournaments happening, a women's tourney and a men's tourney, so I went to both.

At the women's tournament, I found a good vantage point behind the first green. I could sit and watch the ladies approach the first hole and putt. Then I could see them tee off for the second hole. I didn't have to follow the crowds and players around the golf course. I recognized a few names of the female golfers. One lady at the first hole made a bad chip and three-putted for a double bogey, two over par. The scorekeeper showed her score as one over par which was an error.

Another young lady played to the first green and one-putted for a birdie, one under par. An elderly couple behind me were talking about how well she did so I asked if they were family. They said they were providing the young lady with living accommodations for the week of the tournament. Evidently golf courses reach out to local residents prior to PGA events to find free living quarters for golfers in financial need. It sounded like a great plan to me and this elderly couple were both excited to have the young lady staying with them. They were following her around the golf course.

I watched the men's tournament from the same vantage point, and there were some famous players there. I remember seeing Chi Chi Rodriguez, Lee Trevino, Jack Nicklaus, Arnold Palmer, and even ex-president Gerald Ford. The men's tournament was a pro/am event and Gerald Ford had secret service men driving his golf cart. All the famous golfers had a security guard dressed in black walking beside them during their rounds.

Watching the two pro tournaments was entertaining. I didn't see many bad golf shots. The pros made the game of golf look easy.

Golf Hole-In-One

I took up golf in high school and played through my college years. My scoring was bogey ball; I seldom shot a par round of golf. After college I traveled and worked so my golf clubs disappeared. Only occasionally, when I visited family, did I get out on a golf course.

After retiring, I bought a set of used golf clubs and started hitting practice balls again. I moved to Fresno, CA, and began playing a short par 3 golf course there. My swing slowly improved and my scores were between bogey and par.

For three years I played that short par 3 golf course in Fresno and managed to get four hole-in-ones there. One was memorable. I teed off at a green 140 yards away and pulled the ball left out of bounds. So I teed up another ball and hit a second shot into a white, cloudy sky. I didn't see the ball but the swing and contact felt good. I walked to the green and looked all around. There was no ball on the green or in the rough grass around the green. When I looked in the hole, there was the ball. About four feet in front of the hole was a fresh divot. It was a perfect shot.

So I got a hole-in-one, but my score for the hole was three strokes which is par. My first shot out of bounds added up to one swinging stroke plus one penalty stroke. My next tee shot went in the hole. So I had two swinging strokes and a penalty stroke for a par 3 on the hole. That doesn't happen very often.

The next golf course that I tried in Fresno is a short par 4 course. It has five par 3 greens and four short par 4 greens. I played there for three years and managed five hole-in-ones on that course. One was memorable.

One of the par 4 holes on that course has woods on the left, flat dirt on the right, and a sand trap across two-thirds of the front of the green. I teed up my ball at 190 yards from the green and hit a driver. The ball went straight, just missing the sand trap. It was a very good shot. I walked to the green and saw no golf ball. It wasn't in front or back or to the sides of the green. So it could only be in one place. I walked to the hole and there it was. A hole-in-one on a par 4 hole.

Getting a hole-in-one on a par 4 green is very rare. So rare, in fact, that the odds are like matching DNA numbers. I may be the first Willis on planet Earth to have made a hole-in-one on a par 4 golf green since the origin of golf. Many golfers have gotten a hole-in-one on a par 3 green, but few golfers have even heard of someone getting a hole-in-one on a par 4 green. It is a blue-moon event.

My golf game today has moved to a different 18-hole golf course close to my home. It's a challenging course for short hitters like me. I'm still playing bogey ball and don't take my golf game or my scores too seriously. Golf has become my daily exercise.

Vegas Sports

Las Vegas loves sporting events and sports teams. Metro Las Vegas is now large enough to accommodate professional sports teams.

When I was traveling, I passed through Vegas numerous times. One of my stops there had the U.S. women's Olympic volleyball team playing against China at one of the casinos. My game ticket was inexpensive. It was a three-game match and both teams were high in the world rankings. I was much impressed with both teams; those ladies could play volleyball. They were tall, fast, and could slam, serve, and dig. The U.S. team won the match but it was a close contest.

That same trip I went to a men's professional tennis tournament in Vegas. I don't recall where it was played but the tourney was hosted by comedian Alan King. I saw parts of the tennis action on two different days. Jimmy Connors was there playing; I walked past him at the tennis courts but didn't see any of his matches. During one match, something interesting happened. I was sitting in the stands facing the baseline, and a tennis shot landed inches past the baseline in foul territory. The line judge called the ball out which was the correct call. The referee sitting high in a chair by the net saw otherwise and called the ball fair. In a loud voice, I spoke up and declared the ball out of bounds by six inches. The referee heard me and looked at where I was sitting, then changed his call. He called the ball a "let" which means replay the point. So the two players replayed the point.

Following the tournament there was a prize ceremony. Alan King handed out paychecks to winners. I didn't know many of the tennis players there other than Jimmy Connors. The tournament winner I didn't recognize.

Today Las Vegas has a number of casinos with coliseums big enough for major sporting events. And the city now has huge stadiums for professional sports teams. Sports and gambling go hand in hand as Vegas continues to grow.

Famous Boxer

Years ago when I was traveling, I spent some time in Las Vegas. Boxing was happening at one of the casinos so I bought a cheap seat. It was a regional amateur boxing tournament, early 1980s, and I sat through all the bouts. In one of the heavier divisions the announcer introduced Evander Holyfield as one of the boxers, saying he was a good fighter. Most people, including myself, had never heard of him.

The bell sounded for the first round and the opponent, a big muscled white guy, came out swinging. He almost ran toward Holyfield, throwing punches with both hands. His strategy was obvious: be first with his punches and land the early blows. Holyfield wasn't hurt by the flurry; he threw one uppercut which landed and the opponent dropped face down on the floor. The fight was over in about thirty seconds.

When the next summer Olympics came, I remembered the name because Holyfield won a bronze medal. After the Olympics he turned pro and in 1986 he won the world cruiserweight title. Then he moved up to heavyweight and won the world heavyweight championship in 1990. He fought professionally until 2014 and by then everyone had heard of Evander Holyfield.

Bowling

After I retired at age 62, I started doing some fun things. I took trips to Las Vegas and Reno. I ate at restaurants, went bowling, played miniature golf, attended sports games, went to concerts and movies, played golf. It was so nice not having a work schedule.

I took a lady out to eat and afterward we went bowling. During our game, she stepped to the line with her bowling ball and strode forward. As she released the ball, her front foot slipped and she fell on her butt, sliding part way down the alley. I was watching this new style of bowling and looked to my right to see if anybody was watching. A group of bowlers far to the right were occupied with their game. I looked left and bowlers at that end of the bowling rink didn't see it. I looked behind me and the employees at the fee counter were busy with other things. The only two people in the bowling alley who had seen her fall were me and her.

She got up totally embarrassed. She couldn't believe what she'd just done. I told her the good news; nobody in the place had seen it happen except me and her, so no worries. I picked up my bowling ball and rolled it and said no more about the mishap. She felt somewhat relieved knowing that others hadn't seen her fall.

Another time I went bowling with a lady I knew well. She had on a pair of used bowling shoes purchased from Ebay. In the middle of our game, she stepped to the line with a ball in her hand. As she walked forward, her right heel moved upward from her toe and the rubber tread on the bottom of her shoe peeled off. I'm watching as she walked out of the bottom of her bowling shoe. She strode forward and released the bowling ball, then looked down at her feet. Something didn't feel right. Half her shoe was on her foot and the other half was back at the starting line. Too funny.

Home Run

I've seen a play in a baseball game that almost never happens, maybe once in fifty years. I was there on game day and saw it with my own eyes.

Fresno State University was playing a home baseball game against another California college. It was late innings in the game, maybe the eighth inning, and the other team came to bat. Fresno State was leading 5-2, and the other team managed to get runners on first and second bases with one out. The next batter hit a fastball so hard that the ball was still rising when it cleared the center field fence. It was a monster home run. The runner at second base trotted to third and on to home base for a score. The runner at first base was so impressed by the distance of the homer that he walked toward second base and then stopped near the outfield grass, looking to see where the ball landed. He wasn't yet to second base.

The batter, after hitting the ball, knew immediately it was a homer so he tossed his bat aside and began trotting to first base at a rapid clip. His head was down as he rounded first base and continued toward second base. When he stepped on second base, somebody shouted at him. He looked back and saw the first-base runner still standing between first and second bases.

Seeing that he had run ahead of the runner at first base, the batter realized that he was out when he touched second base. Without trying to argue his mistake, he trotted a half circle toward his team's dugout and left the field. He knew he was out and everybody else did, too. The baserunner standing between first and second bases finished running to second, third, and home base for his score.

Now the game score was 5-4 in favor of Fresno State, and there were two outs in the inning. The next batter came to the plate, but the opposing team couldn't score another run.

And that's how the game ended, with Fresno State winning 5-4. The news write-up after the game was about the home run that didn't count as a home run.

Taco Contest

I was at the ball game the day this happened. The Fresno minor league baseball team was hosting a home game. A friend and I were in the bleachers. Halfway through the game the announcer said there would be a taco-eating contest about to begin. Several participants were selected from the crowd. The person who could eat the most tacos in a few minutes would win a prize.

I'd been to other Fresno Grizzlies baseball games that had a taco or hotdog-eating contest, so this wasn't new. What was new this time was that we didn't hear any more from the announcer about the taco contest. No winner was announced.

My friend and I drove home after the game and the next day I heard the news. One of the taco-eating contestants had choked to death. Medical people responded to the scene but couldn't open the guy's airway in time.

That incident happened three years ago, and I recently heard news that a settlement with the family was nearing a closure. No doubt the final price tag will be megabucks. Needless to say, the Fresno Grizzlies baseball games no longer have eating contests.

Dad's War Stories

My dad recounted a few of his WW2 stories to our family. When the U.S. entered the second world war, dad left college and enlisted in military flight training. One evening he went on a date with a sister of one of his flight classmates. The date went well and the two exchanged letters during the war. After Japan surrendered, dad went to see Helene Jensen and proposed to her. They were married soon after.

Dad's pilot training was not easy. There were many ways a pilot could wash out, and some trainees were killed during flight training. On one training exercise, dad was flying with a squad of airplanes, each carrying a heavy bomb. One of the pilots moved his controls wrong and accidentally turned his plane upside down at low altitude. The pilot tried to recover by pulling out underneath but the plane hit the ground.

Another novice pilot was approaching a landing with his wheels up so the instructor ran to the middle of the runway. The pilot was forced to pull up and observers assumed he would realize something was wrong. The pilot circled and came in for another landing, wheels still up, skidding along the runway for quite a distance. The punishment for such a mistake was meant to be memorable and embarrassing. The pilot was required to carry an airplane undercarriage bar everywhere he went for a certain number of days.

Dad spent his war years in the Pacific theater flying dive bombers. On one occasion he witnessed a plane taxi to a parking area in front of a control tower. As the plane circled toward the control building, the pilot accidentally squeezed the gun trigger. Bullets ripped into the control building with people inside. Dad didn't hear the outcome but he didn't think there were injuries.

One flight mission had my dad and three other pilots flying dive bombers to a Japanese-held island. Their objective was to bomb a suspicious target seen from aerial photographs. They made a bombing run over that target and the plane behind dad's dropped the bomb that scored a hit on a camouflaged fuel depot.

When General Douglas MacArthur gathered his naval fleet for the invasion of the Philippines in 1944, dad was flying submarine patrol off the island of Ulithi. Dad said he had full view of MacArthur's fleet which stretched as far as the eye could see.

The saddest war story that dad told me was about a young pilot in his Pacific flight squadron. The fellow got news from his wife in the states that he was a father; she'd given birth to a healthy baby boy. The young pilot hosted a party for all the airmen and passed out cigars. He was feeling proud. A few days later he tried a stunt in his airplane which was forbidden by the commander. He tried to fly his airplane underneath a bridge to see if he could do it and crashed.

Civil War Sword

"**A**ntiques Roadshow" on PBS television, both the American and the United Kingdom series, are entertaining. The antique experts in both series are very good. Civil War artifacts are sometimes brought to the Roadshow, and when I see an expert talk about a US Civil War sword, it brings back memories. Our Willis family once had an authentic Civil War sword. It sat by the fireplace in our big white house in Marshalltown, Iowa.

One of my distant grandfathers had fought for the Union in the Civil War. During a battle, he was wearing the sword and it was hit by a bullet which left a large dent in the scabbard. After the war, that grandfather named one of his sons Ulysses S. Grant Willis, and his dented sword was passed down through generations of the family. My father ended up with it.

I was about ten years old when that sword disappeared from our home. It somehow got lost or thrown away. Not until my later years, when I started watching "Antiques Roadshow", did I remember the sword. Having a bullet dent in the scabbard would have made for interesting conversation with a Roadshow expert. That sword had value. As an elder now, I feel bad that our family didn't take better care of that sword. It was a fine Willis relic and worthy of keeping in the family.

Biped Food

I like television documentaries. Educational documentaries are good for the brain, and several that I've seen have changed my life. A few years ago I watched a documentary about bipeds and the food they eat. Bipeds are animals that walk on two feet, like you and me, and the first bipeds were monkeys walking on the ground. The TV show emphasized that humans evolved from biped monkeys, and both monkeys and humans have always been plant eaters. The shape of the jaws and teeth in monkeys and humans is for eating plants, not for ripping meat. For the last three million years monkeys and humans have been getting most of their needed food nutrition from plants.

Scientists in the documentary showed that people who eat only plant foods have clean, transparent blood. People who eat plant foods plus meat and dairy products have dark, murky blood. Clean blood is better for the body, and plant foods provide the human body with all the necessary vital nutrients. Eating only plant foods doesn't cause any loss of physical strength, energy, or sexual prowess.

Arnold Schwarzenegger, the bodybuilder, has now embraced the vegetarian path. He estimates plant foods are now 80% of his diet. I've changed my diet the same way. I still drink nonfat milk but don't eat much meat anymore. I see vegetarians in a new light now.

Stone Mountain and the Atlanta 500

Stone Mountain is fifteen miles east of Atlanta, GA, and visible for many miles. I drove there after viewing it from a freeway. It's a state park with numerous attractions, including shops and motels for overnight visitors. The big attraction is the mountain itself. It is a giant rock monolith, with carvings of three huge figures on horseback: Confederate President Jefferson Davis, General Thomas "Stonewall" Jackson, and General Robert E. Lee. The rock sculptures are massive, something like Mount Rushmore in South Dakota. Today there is growing criticism about the three Confederate leaders portrayed in the statues, but the carvings are a marvel to see.

I stayed overnight at Stone Mountain and the next day drove to the Atlanta Motor Speedway. I wanted to see the Atlanta 500 NASCAR race. This would be a first for me. Before race time I drove my motorhome into the center of the oval track where scores of other vehicles were parked. I was amazed at how steep the racetrack is from side to side. Television doesn't show the steep angle that a racetrack really has.

The weather was good on race day and the stadium seats were nearly full. The center of the oval track was filled with cars and spectators, and everybody was hyped for the start of the race. A couple of dozen race cars got lined up on the track and a pace car and flagman finally got them all started. Some of the driver's names I knew. Around and around the roaring cars went. The noise was loud and before long the cars were making pit stops. Spectators couldn't tell who was in the lead without listening to a radio. There was one accident; near the end of the race a slow car in the rear hit a side wall. After the first fifteen minutes, I was bored and just watching the spectators. The race went on for maybe an hour.

I left the speedway knowing that I wouldn't need to see another NASCAR auto race. One was enough for me. A week later I was watching television and guess what was on: the Atlanta 500. Most viewers didn't know that the race had happened a week earlier. This was a replay, and I knew who was going to win the race.

Bad Brakes

After working for a month on a St. Paul riverboat, I pointed my motorhome eastward. I drove into the hills of Tennessee and noticed I was having brake problems. What I didn't know was that an oil seal inside one of my rear wheels was leaking oil. I came to the top of a highway hill and at the bottom was a car off road. A female park ranger was standing there with her arms raised, signaling for me to stop. I pushed hard on my brakes but couldn't stop on the down slope. The only thing that saved me from a serious accident was that there were no other vehicles stopped in front of me. I was forced to keep on driving.

After that close call, I continued driving east using my automatic transmission gears for slowing down when needed. It was apparent that my brakes were bad so I began traveling on flat freeways through North Carolina. When I reached the ocean, I turned south along the Outer Banks. While driving that highway, I got a strong premonition about checking the wheels on my RV. Could there be something wrong with my wheels? I pulled off the highway and did a walkaround. My right rear dual wheel had two lug nuts broken off, and two of the three remaining lug nuts were loose. So I got a wrench and tightened all the lug nuts on all the wheels. Then I turned around and drove slowly back to the nearest city thirty miles away. It took me two days to get the broken lug bolts on my RV replaced. It was another close call.

From North Carolina I turned back toward the Midwest. When I got to St. Paul, I took my motorhome to an auto repair shop for a brake inspection. What I learned was no surprise; I had no brakes. All the brake shoes and pads were worn out. One brake seal was leaking oil onto a brake hub. I needed new brake cylinders and new brake shoes all around. That was a major repair job. I'd driven through the Tennessee Smoky Mountains without brakes.

After the brake repair was finished, my RV was safe to drive again. I did another month of work on a St. Paul riverboat and then headed east across Canada.

Broken Nose

I know what a broken nose looks like and feels like. In high school I took an elbow to my nose during a touch football game. I went to the hospital expecting some kind of surgery. Instead, a doctor sat down in a chair in front of me and pushed my nose back in place as best he could. Then he taped a protective brace over it.

A couple of days later I took the nose guard off to see how it looked. To my dismay, my nose was still bent to one side, so I began pushing it straight myself. Then I taped the guard back on, pressing it against my nose in the direction that looked straight. A week later I removed the nose guard again to take another look. This time my nose was almost straight which was a big relief.

Many years later I was working in California at Lake Kaweah and received a radio call in the office. There was an injury at one of the recreation areas. I drove there to find a small boy, about four years old, with his nose pushed badly to one side. It looked ugly and he was crying his eyes out. His family was there and his mother was in hysterics. She wanted somebody to come and fix her boy's nose right away.

I got a flashlight and looked inside the boy's nose. There was no bleeding anywhere, inside or out. So I told the father, who was relatively composed, that the best and fastest way to get his son's nose fixed was to drive him to the hospital. Nobody at Lake Kaweah could perform nose surgery. The boy wasn't bleeding so he wasn't in jeopardy.

The father thought for a moment, then ordered his family into the car. In short order he was on the road, headed for town. In the distance I could hear the wail of a siren coming our way. A reserve sheriff deputy, there on scene, had called for emergency medical services. Seeing the father drive away, he got back on his radio and cancelled the EMS request.

Here was a case where the solution to a medical problem was obvious. The boy wasn't bleeding so drive him to a hospital for emergency care. It was faster than an ambulance without the added costs of emergency medical services. But not one single person at that injury scene had thought of it. Everybody there was looking for an ambulance ASAP.

Pork BBQ

One summer at Lake Kaweah in California, the lake was low and the campground began getting unwanted visitors at night. A group of wild pigs began rooting after dark. This continued for a week. One morning the campground hosts could see the pigs not far away so we called the local sheriff deputy. We told him the problem, and bring a gun.

The sheriff deputy showed up and drove as close to the pigs as he could. He wanted to shoot the leader, a big black boar, but it got nervous and started trotting in the direction of a distant road. So he changed his aim and squeezed the trigger on a smaller sow. The herd bolted off, following the black boar. We didn't see those pigs anywhere near the Kaweah campground again that summer. The rooting problem was solved.

The sheriff deputy made a call on his radio after he shot the pig. He told the local Fish and Game Warden that he needed to talk to him about a red-head with pigtails. I heard the call.

Several days later a notice was posted at the Lake Kaweah office. There was a barbeque planned. Everybody paid a few dollars for food. On barbeque day, some housewives arrived with an assortment of food and drinks. Somebody brought the pig which had been dressed out. Everybody was there: the Lake Kaweah staff and wives, Kaweah boat patrol, the campground hosts, the sheriff deputy. Even the Fish and Game Warden was there. The food was good and the barbeque went well; it was a fun occasion.

Christmas Trees

When I worked at Eastman Lake in California, our ranger staff sometimes transported Christmas trees to the lake for fish habitat. Residents in a nearby city would discard their Christmas trees after the holidays at several locations, and our Eastman staff would truck some of those trees to the lake. Somewhere near the water we would cable the trees together and affix them to the ground, using volunteers, scouts, and staff for the work. In the Spring, when the water level rose, the submerged trees provided shelter and habitat for small fish.

One winter a student ranger brought a truck load of trees to the lake. I met him in a flat area where we wanted to build some fish habitat. A female ranger drove up and began walking around the area. The student ranger said he might be able to slide the trees out of the truck box, so we dropped the rear gate door. He drove the truck forward, put the truck in reverse, revved the engine, and began a fast reverse. His intention was to make a sudden stop and have the trees slide out of the rear truck box.

The student ranger didn't know there was another ranger on scene. He didn't see the female ranger wandering around on foot. I began walking toward the drop area as he was backing up, and then I saw the lady ranger. She was standing in the flats behind the truck, looking down at the ground, not paying attention. I yelled at her and she looked up. Just in the nick of time she jumped to the side as the rear truck gate sped past her. The height of the rear truck gate was about the height of her neck and head. Had she been hit, she would have been killed.

After seeing this happen, I was in a state of shock. My whole body began trembling. The student driver didn't know anything had happened because he never saw the other ranger. He made a sudden stop but the trees didn't slide out of the rear truck box. The female who narrowly missed death realized her carelessness but didn't say anything. She recovered from the scare fairly quickly and left the scene. But for me, it was a different story. I had seen how close that lady came to death, and I'm talking only a few seconds.

Over the next several weeks my brain continued to replay that scene over and over in my mind. I didn't calm down for maybe a month, thinking about the possible consequences. The relief I felt after that incident stretched on and on for weeks and months and still stays with me today.

Freezing Cold

I was working on a riverboat on the St. Paul waterway in wintertime. The temperature had dropped to 25 degrees below zero when I got off the boat. My motorhome was parked near the company maintenance compound and it wouldn't start. The engine was too cold. I slept in the RV at nights, waiting for the weather to warm up, but the freeze continued. A small portable water cooler was my water supply, and my meals were cans of soup. At night inside my RV the heater was on full blast and I turned on the stove flames but it was still freezing cold. Wrapped in thermal clothes and blankets, my body was shivering in the middle of the night.

Finally I talked to some company maintenance workers who told me to put a frost plug heater on my engine block. They said it wasn't expensive or difficult to install and once plugged into electricity, the engine coolant would warm up. So I got a ride to an auto parts store and bought a frost plug heater. After reading the instructions, I dressed for the cold and got under my motorhome. I tapped loose one frost plug on the engine block and out came antifreeze which I tried to catch in a pan. Then I carefully reinserted the newly purchased heater plug. Following instructions, I tightened the new heater plug in place. So far, so good.

Everything looked in order so I refilled the motorhome radiator with antifreeze. Then I plugged a long electric cord into the heater plug. It all worked as planned. There were no fluid leaks around the heater plug and the engine antifreeze warmed up. I cleaned up everything and put a key in the ignition. The outside temperature was still 20 degrees below zero but the engine started immediately. I put it in gear and drove south to Marshalltown, Iowa where I had family and friends.

In Marshalltown, I discovered that the drinking water system in my RV needed repair. A frozen water pipe had broken so I fixed that. After spending several weeks with family and friends in Iowa, I headed south toward warmer climate.

Soul Travel and Dream Travel

I was thirty years old when I first learned about the phenomenon of out-of-body travel. I read a book that said every person has this capability. Amazed by this claim, I decided to give it a try. I tried concentrating at bedtime for a couple of weeks but nothing happened. Then one evening I managed to shift above my physical self into a world of blackness. I wasn't sure what happened but it was real. After that I continued my nightly concentration efforts, trying to learn some way of projecting out of body regularly. My progress was slow but I managed an occasional OBE. After a year I had a diary of enough OBEs to begin writing a book.

Those early projections sometimes gave me a feeling of separating from my physical form, which made them feel real. I sometimes ended up in the Earth environment, but more often I ended up in a nonphysical world somewhere. The inner worlds that I visited looked dreamlike, but I could touch things around me, including my soul body.

As time passed, my OBEs began to change. After contemplating in the middle of the night and drifting into sleep, I would suddenly become conscious of already being out of body in an inner world. If my conscious awareness was good, I would know and understand what was happening. But if my conscious awareness was poor, the experience could seem dreamlike afterward. Was it a dream or an OBE?

Today I view "soul travel" as a soul body separating and moving away from the physical form. Whether the soul body ends up in the Earth environment or an inner world somewhere, an experience like this will feel authentic. But out-of-body travel can happen differently. "Dream travel" is what I call an instantaneous shift into the inner planes. Dream travel will seem real if conscious awareness is good. But if my conscious awareness is poor in the inner worlds, afterward I may wonder if it was a dream because my return will be just as quick.

OBE

I'm going to take you on a dream-travel adventure and give you good conscious awareness. This OBE happened to me years ago so you'll be standing in my shoes. I still remember most of what happened because it was such a strange and vivid experience. I never did figure out what it was all about.

At bedtime this evening you've decided to try and experience an OBE. You're willing to sacrifice some sleep to see if you can project out of your physical body. You set an alarm clock to awaken in four hours' time. Then you go to sleep as usual. When the alarm sounds, you go to the bathroom and relieve any bladder pressure. Then you splash some water on your face to wake yourself up, and go back to bed. If you sleep with a partner, you'll want to go back to bed in a different room that's quiet.

Lie down in bed in your normal sleeping position, close your eyes, and rotate your eyeballs upward. You'll feel a tightness develop about an inch and a half behind the top center of your head. Now mentally pull downward on that feeling of tightness. Next, let your eyeballs rotate downward to a relaxed position while mentally keeping a slight tightness behind the top center of your head. Stay relaxed and continue doing this until you drift into sleep.

Whenever you lose that slight feeling of tightness inside the top center of your head, mentally bring it back and carry on. If you can fall asleep doing this, your chances of projecting out of body automatically are good. It may take an hour, or an hour and a half, or two hours to drift into sleep this way. But stay with it because you're willing to sacrifice some sleep to see if out-of-body travel is possible. This contemplation doesn't have to go smoothly to be successful. Eventually after ninety minutes of doing this, your tiredness puts you to sleep.

Suddenly you become aware of standing in an environment that looks like the southwestern United States. You're surrounded by a panoramic scene of small shrubs and flat sagebrush plains. The sky is soft white, like an evening sky without a sun. As you look around in all directions, there are no other people or manmade objects anywhere in sight. It's only you, standing in the middle of an expanse of sagebrush.

Having good consciousness, you realize what has happened. You've somehow shifted out of your physical body into this world that looks Earthlike. You didn't even feel it happen. Could this be Earth? You're not sure; maybe it's an inner nonphysical world. You look down at your arms and legs and body. You have clothes on and your body feels solid, like the ground you're standing on. Why you're here, how you got here, where this place is, who put you here, it's all a mystery? But you begin to enjoy this feeling of being out of body.

In the distance there's a noise so you look in that direction. Maybe a half mile away, coming over a small hill, are what looks like animals. You realize that a distant herd of cattle are running in your direction, maybe a hundred head. A dust cloud billows around the moving herd, and you begin to feel vibration in the ground. The sound of hooves beating the ground gets louder as the cows run toward you.

Seeing this, you're curious about what's happening? The cattle reach a quarter mile away, still running straight at you. Could there be danger here? With good conscious awareness, you think about where you are, how you got here, and decide not to be afraid. You feel confident that you weren't transported to this place to be trampled by a herd of cattle. That doesn't make sense. So instead of feeling fear in this situation, you put your hands in your pockets and stand firm. With a cocky grin on your face, you feel sure that the cattle won't harm you. Confidence keeps you calm.

On the cows come, still aimed directly at you. The noise gets louder as the distance closes. The ground is shaking and the dust cloud grows. Still you stand motionless, unafraid.

You've chosen not to run. Good consciousness tells you that you'll be okay.

Then the cows arrive and impact comes, but something amazing happens! The lead cow, instead of knocking you to the ground, runs through you! You can feel the cow as it runs through your soul body, even see the cow running through your body. Surprise, surprise! Cattle on both sides race past as the cows in the center of the herd continue running through your body, one after the other. Each cow running through you, you can see and feel it happen. It takes a minute for all the cows to run past you and through you. Still standing motionless, you can hardly believe what's happening. Why and how is a mystery, but you're safe and unharmed. You were right; you weren't brought to this place to be trampled by cows.

Behind you the cows race away, shaking the ground and throwing up dirt. You turn and watch them run off into the distance. Now you're chuckling and laughing. This scary incident turned into a comedy.

As the herd goes distant, you feel a tug, like a magnetic pull on your head and shoulders. Suddenly you're back inside your physical form again, lying in bed. Most of this OBE is still vivid in your mind. Why, how, and where it happened remains a puzzle? Could it have happened somewhere on Earth? You don't have any answers but it was certainly memorable.

I'm going to add a footnote here before ending this story. There are many people around the globe who have experienced and do experience OBEs. I'm going to share some information here that some of these people already know. But for those who don't, they will be happy to learn about it.

After returning from a trip out of body, it is relatively simple and easy to project out of body a second successive time. To do this, all you need to do is remain absolutely, perfectly motionless in bed and go back to sleep. That's it. Don't move any part of your physical body. If you can do this, you will automatically shift out of your physical body into an inner world when you fall asleep. You can do this over and over again the same night. It works automatically, every time. Eventually your physical body will feel uncomfortable and you'll need to shift positions in bed. Once you move any part of your physical body, your free rides into the inner planes are done for the night.

Inner World Languages

Over the past several decades I've had hundreds of out-of-body experiences. Sometimes my out-of-body conscious awareness is good, sometimes not. When I'm in a nonphysical world, I can verbally talk to people and they can talk to me. After returning to my physical body, I usually don't remember much of those conversations, but some of the conversation may stay in my memory.

There are a few things about communication in the inner planes that I know for certain. I know that when I speak the English language to people in the inner planes, they understand what I'm saying and they can talk to me in the same language. I also know for certain that mental telepathy is possible in the inner worlds. I've had OBEs where I was able to communicate with people around me by mentally speaking words in my mind. And they could communicate with me the same way. I'm also certain that while lying in my physical body in bed in a sleep/awake state, I can mentally speak words in my mind that other nonphysical entities can receive and understand (in the English language). This has happened to me a number of times where I found myself lying in bed, asleep physically but awake mentally. Staying motionless, I mentally spoke the words "I want to leave my physical body" and a force then pushed or pulled me out of my physical form.

So my next question is – what about languages in the inner planes? People on Earth don't talk about or think about or write about this. What language or languages are spoken in the inner planes? When I'm out of body in the nonphysical worlds, I talk and communicate in the English language. I've never heard any other language spoken in the inner worlds. But what if I spoke a different language? Could people in the inner worlds understand me? How many languages are spoken in the inner worlds? Can people in the inner worlds speak and understand multiple languages?

Consider the major religions here on Earth that are centered around a particular Savior or Prophet or Godman. Millions of people around the globe are devoted to these spiritual giants. But how do these Saviors, Prophets, and Godmen understand and communicate with so many followers of so many different languages?

I am totally at a loss to the question about languages in the inner planes. After I die here on Earth, will I shift into the inner worlds and communicate only in the English language? Or will I somehow be able to communicate in other languages as well? If so, how did I learn the other languages? Do other people in the inner worlds speak only one language, or multiple languages, or all languages? If people in the inner worlds can speak all languages, how did they learn this?

Try this possibility. Could there be English-speaking areas in the inner worlds, plus other areas in the inner worlds for people speaking other languages? Sound crazy or silly? Sure does. But the question still begs, does anybody have an answer?

Sleep, Dreams, and More

A couple of years ago I developed a nagging back pain and began having trouble sleeping at night. This was something new for me because I've never had back pain and always been a sound sleeper. Then one morning while changing my bed sheets, I realized that my mattress had a large sag in the middle of it. I wasn't sleeping on a level surface. Could this be the reason for my back pain and lack of sleep?

So I went to my computer and purchased a BedInABox mattress. A week later it was delivered. Watching it pop out of the packaging box and slowly rise up was interesting. I put the mattress on my bed and now had a flat cushion to sleep on. My back pain went away and my sleep returned to normal.

Most nights for me will bring lots of colored dream activity. If I'm in a light sleep, my dreams will be two dimensional. I'll see an assortment of pictures in my subconscious mind. If I'm in a deep sleep, my dreams can be three dimensional. I'll be participating in some kind of activity, maybe with a solid body, but my conscious mind won't be there. My activity will be guided by my subconscious mind. Some of my deep dreams likely happen in the inner worlds, but afterward I won't remember much about them.

Much research has been done about dreams over the past several decades. Doctors, scientists, and researchers have now concluded that dreams are good and even necessary for people. Dreams can help a person's mental and physical well-being. Deep dreaming can now be measured electronically, and everyone apparently experiences deep REM dreams nightly. The subconscious mind is the principal player during these deep dreams. Consciously we don't need to know what deep dreams mean or how they help us.

From past experiences I can recall a number of times when I felt sick at bedtime, maybe a head sickness or a body sickness. After contemplating in the middle of the night and projecting out of my physical body with consciousness, I later returned to find that my physical body was feeling well. My sickness had somehow disappeared. So I do believe that nighttime dreaming, especially deep dreams, can be beneficial for the brain and body.

I recall an OBE which readers here will find interesting. I was out of body one night in a solid soul body with good conscious awareness. A person with me reached out to touch my hand, and the arm of that person passed through my physical body which was lying on my bed. I could feel that person's arm penetrate into and through my physical head. What that meant was that even though I couldn't see my physical self, my soul body was close to it.

Probably many of my deep, active REM dreams happen in the inner worlds, either inside or close to my physical body. This could be true for many of my conscious dream travels as well. The inner worlds are tuned to higher energy levels than this Earth environment, so all of these worlds can occupy the same area of space. Out-of-body travel can happen close to or far from the physical body.

Death

Out-of-body experiences have changed my view of death. When I was young, the thought of dying terrified me. But I don't feel that strong fear of death anymore. I'm still afraid to die. If a bad guy pointed a gun at me, I'd be diving for cover like anybody else. But my OBEs have tempered my fear of dying.

What's more important for me is that I'm now certain there is life after death. Many times while out of my physical body, I've consciously thought about how physical death doesn't end a person's life. Someday when my time comes here on Earth and my family members cremate my physical body, I'll be somewhere else, in some inner world somewhere, doing something. It's comforting for me to know this, that physical death won't be the end of me.

The Subconscious Mind

I decided to include several stories about out-of-body travel in this book but wasn't sure what to say. So I gave that question to my subconscious mind. First, I reviewed two soul-travel books that I've written and published. Then I mulled over that information, wondering what I could write for the general public. After some thought, I let the matter rest.

For the next several days and nights my subconscious mind went to work. During sleep I could see paragraphs of words scrolling on my inner mind screen. While sleeping, I sometimes heard my own voice inside my head, talking about soul travel. After a few days of letting my subconscious roll, I began to see stories emerge. I would write about (1) Soul Travel and Dream Travel, (2) OBE, and (3) Death. Then it was just a matter of roughing out each story and rewriting until polished.

Letting the subconscious mind solve issues and problems is something everyone can do. The subconscious is made for this. If you've got a problem to figure out, or a task to perform, or a decision to make, or a plan that's needed, let your subconscious mind help you. It's simple and easy to do. Just review in your mind all the pertinent data and facts. Then consider the different angles of approach. Think about what's good, bad, easy, hard, practical, people involved, timeline, money, etc. After taking a 360 degree look at the problem or issue, let it go. Give your subconscious mind some time to figure out an answer.

Within a few days a solution will pop into your brain, like a light bulb being turned on. Your best answer will become obvious. You may wonder why you didn't think of it before. Now you can move forward and make it happen.

Hypnotism and Motion Sickness

I started this life as a bed-wetter. My bed-wetting continued for several years and my mom grew increasingly frustrated. Finally she took me to a doctor who specialized in hypnosis therapy and told him the problem. The doctor sat me down in a chair and had me close my eyes. Then in a monotone voice he explained what he wanted me to do. He told me to wake up in the middle of the night and go to the bathroom, then go back to bed. I didn't feel hypnotized; I was just listening to him talk. After he finished, he had me open my eyes. It only lasted a few minutes.

That evening my mom and dad invited friends over for a late card game because they wanted to see what would happen. Mom told me later that about midnight I got out of bed and walked to the bathroom. She followed me and found me standing in front of the toilet, but I was turned around facing the wall. She rushed in when I started peeing on the wall and got me turned around, aimed at the toilet. Then she cleaned me up, put me in bed, and cleaned up my bathroom mess. The next morning I didn't remember anything about getting out of bed in the night or going to the bathroom.

In the following days I did better about getting out of bed in the night and going to the bathroom. The doctor had scheduled a follow-up appointment, so a week later mom and I went to see him again. The doctor sat me down in a chair and had me close my eyes. In a monotone voice he said I was a good boy and I was to wake up in the night and go to the bathroom and pee in the toilet and then go back to bed.

After that, my bed-wetting problem went away. In the middle of the night, I would get up and go to the bathroom like I was supposed to. My mother was so impressed with how quickly my bed-wetting stopped that I remember her telling other people about it. Hypnosis works.

And there's more to this hypnosis story. I grew up and went through high school and then on to college. During my college years, I sometimes went to bars with friends. Some college city bars have stage shows, and the first hypnosis show that I saw in a bar turned out educational for me. The hypnotist asked for volunteers from the audience to come up on stage. I didn't volunteer. A number of volunteers got seated on a stage and the hypnotist began talking to them in a monotone voice. Right away I noticed that I was getting hypnotized in the back of the audience, so I got out of my chair and went outside. I had to walk around outside and shake myself for a few minutes to clear my head. This happened to me more than once so I learned that I'm very susceptible to being hypnotized.

Motion sickness was another problem for me when I was young. I often got car sick when riding in a car so my mother took me to an eye doctor. My eyesight was bad so I had to wear thick glasses. But even with glasses, I was still susceptible to motion sickness. At fairs I didn't like the rides because I got dizzy, even on easy rollercoaster rides. And that's still true for me today. I've always marveled at how airplane pilots can handle motion and gravity forces because my brain can't do it.

Eyewear

My older sister and I were born very near-sighted. Both of us wore thick glasses growing up. My mom went to see a doctor to find out why her children couldn't see well and she was diagnosed with Vitamin B deficiency. She began taking vitamin B shots for a time and the rest of her children were born with good vision.

As a youngster wearing thick glasses, I was never one of the "cool, popular" kids in school. Girls weren't interested in boys with thick glasses and I wasn't part of the popular crowd through junior high school. I finally made a change to hard contact lenses in senior high. It was difficult, though. The hard contacts were painful for me, especially at the beginning, but I stayed with it because I hated thick glasses. Slowly I got more accustomed to hard contacts. Wearing time for hard contacts was only ten hours a day, however. Any more than that and my eyes would get sore and red. I stayed with hard lenses through my college years.

Then came the soft contact revolution. That changed my life for the better. The eye doctor didn't recommend soft lenses for me because he said the lenses would be large and thick and my vision wouldn't be sharp. I told him I didn't care; I had suffered long enough with hard contacts. I wanted to try soft contact lenses.

The new soft contacts worked fine for me. I couldn't see 20/20 but my vision was close to that and I could wear the lenses sixteen hours a day. They weren't painful. For reading, I used reading glasses. I stayed with soft lenses for the next thirty-five years.

Prior to retirement I started considering Lasik surgery, which reshapes the curvature of the eyes. Maybe I would have this done after I retired. When I did retire, another better option emerged. Corneal transplants cost about the same as

Lasik surgery. Many older people need corneal transplants because of cloudy vision. Having a corneal transplant could correct my near-sightedness and avoid the cloudy lens problem. So I went with corneal transplants.

Surgery was performed on one eye at a time and the total cost for me was about $6,000 without insurance. My vision afterward was/is good, not 20/20, but I can now see about 20/35. I wear reading glasses when needed. I'm now watching sports games in my retirement years with vision close to normal.

Kit Carson

I watched a television series awhile back about young kids and reincarnation. A boy two years old was having recurring nightmares and couldn't sleep. When he first began to talk, he would tell his mother about the same nightmare he was having each night. He would see a man being killed, then the wife and daughter of the man were both killed, and then their bodies were burned. He was the one who killed them and burned their bodies. He didn't like going to sleep because he would see this same scene over and over.

The mother began to wonder if there could be a reincarnation connection to the frightening dreams. She asked the boy questions as he grew. By the time the boy was 5 or 6 years old she had learned more about the bad dreams. The boy said he was a young soldier in the dream, and he had mistakenly killed an important man who looked like an Indian. The young soldier was told by an officer to kill the man's wife and daughter so nobody would know. He did this and then burned the bodies to get rid of any evidence. Afterwards the young soldier was tormented by guilt for the rest of his life.

The boy finally came up with a name. He said the young soldier's name was Kit. The mother searched on the computer and found an explorer/soldier named Kit Carson. She showed the picture of Kit Carson to the boy and he said "yes", that was him.

No historian or writer of Kit Carson lore has ever written anything about this story mentioned above. If true, this would be a new Kit Carson story, something not known before. Kit Carson has always been described as a respected frontiersman, explorer, and soldier who was involved in Indian affairs and Indian wars during the middle 1800s. All the native tribes of the southwest U.S. knew of Carson, in particular the Navajo and Utes.

Clovis Activities

I'm now retired in Clovis, CA, which is part of metropolitan Fresno. For exercise, I golf on weekdays. For entertainment, I follow Fresno State college sports teams. My mobile home park is located close to everything: shopping centers, post office, banking, golf course, movie theaters, restaurants, etc. Three miles away is Fresno State University which has football, basketball, baseball, softball, and other sports teams.

Adjacent to the college is a large auditorium, Save Mart Center, which seats 13,000 people. Save Mart has become a busy hub for sporting events and shows of all kinds. I've seen many college basketball games at Save Mart Center. Other attractions there include Monster Truck Jams, professional bull riding, WWE wrestling, and music concerts aplenty. Bon Jovi was probably the best rock concert I've seen at Save Mart Center to date. The Willie Nelson show surprised me. I went to see Alison Kraus who opened the show, but Willie and his family were just as good. I stay abreast of what's happening at Save Mart Center and if the price is right, I'll go.

The Clovis senior center isn't far from where I live. It's a nice facility with activities and inexpensive meals for seniors. Each summer, beginning in mid-May, free music concerts are held in a grass park in front of the senior center. Different music groups perform on Friday evenings and the public is invited. The music is varied but mainly blue grass and country western. The bands are entertaining and most of the audience are seniors.

There's also a Fresno radio station that sponsors free rock-and-roll concerts during the summer months. Different rock bands are scheduled to play at a shopping mall near the Fresno State College. The public is invited and the bands are good.

Every Spring, Clovis has a rodeo which opens with a parade and spans five days, drawing large crowds of people. Through the summer months the city of Clovis hosts a Farmer's Market every Friday evening. Downtown streets are blocked off for foot traffic and an outdoor band plays music.

So there are inexpensive things to do for seniors in Clovis.

Shopping Spree

A senior lady who I know in Clovis, CA, has several great grandchildren. Not long ago I offered two of them a shopping trip. Their great grandmother and I would take them to a store and each of them could buy any three items in the store that they wanted. I didn't tell them it would happen at a Dollar Store. Both young girls liked the idea so my friend set a date and we took her car.

At the Dollar Store we went inside and I gave each girl a plastic bag. They could search through the store and pick out any three items that they wanted. There was no time schedule; they could take as much time as they wanted. So off they went; one was nine years old and the other six. I grabbed a store basket and began shopping for myself. I collected some things that I needed, paid for them at the counter, and then sat down in the front of the store with my friend.

About ten minutes later the two girls showed up, each with their three items. I gave the nine-year-old a five-dollar bill and told her to pay at the counter. I took the sack of items from the six-year-old and told her I would hold it for her. She was to go through the pay line with her older cousin and watch how to pay. The two girls got in the pay line and when their turn came, the nine-year-old put her items on the counter, gave five dollars to the clerk, and received some change which she brought to me.

Then I gave the six-year-old her sack of items along with a five-dollar bill and told her to do the same. She got in the counter line and when it came her turn, she put her items on the counter, gave the cashier the five-dollar bill, and turned and smiled and waved at me. The cashier gave her some change which she promptly ran and gave to me. The cashier put her three items in the sack and then called for her to come back and get the stuff she bought. The youngster ran back to the counter, grabbed her sack, then ran back to me and gave me a high-five hand slap.

From there we drove down the street to a restaurant. We went inside and everybody ordered a meal. I asked the girls about who would pay for their meals since the food wasn't free. Both of them pointed their finger at me so I told the waitress to put all the meals on my ticket. Then we discussed the shopping spree. We decided to do another shopping spree in a couple of months, and the next time we would take along a four-year-old sister and let her do some shopping, too.

Chance Encounters

Most people can recall some chance encounters in their lifetime. I remember two, but there were probably more.

During my traveling years, I sometimes drove through Iowa for a home visit. My brother was attending college in Ames, Iowa, so I went there to see him. He didn't know I was coming; this was an unexpected visit. In Ames, I first stopped at a store to buy something before driving to my brother's apartment. Inside the store, I looked around and guess who was there? My brother couldn't believe he was seeing me, and I couldn't believe I was seeing him. What are the odds of that happening?

He told me that while doing school homework in his apartment, he had an impulse to go to that store to purchase something. Inside the store he found his long-lost brother.

Another of my chance encounters happened with a phone call. After retiring from my job at Eastman Lake, I was in Fresno, California and began thinking about some retired folks that I knew. They had been campground hosts at Eastman Lake and we kept in touch after they left. I decided to call them and say hi and find out how they were doing. When the wife picked up the phone, she couldn't believe it was me. She said she was in the middle of writing a letter to me when her phone rang. She didn't need to mail the letter.

Pumping Gas

I was retired, living in Clovis, CA, when this happened. My car needed gas so I drove to a gas station and paid the store clerk $20 for gasoline. I walked back to my car, removed the gas cap, and put the gasoline pump nozzle in my gas tank. Then I got distracted with something for a few minutes before returning to my vehicle. Next I removed the gas pump nozzle from my gas tank and returned it to the gas pump. I put my gas cap back on and drove away.

Down the road I looked at my car's fuel gauge and saw that it was still near empty. How could that be? I just filled the tank. Then I realized what I'd done.

Quickly I turned my car around and drove back to the gas station. Another car was now parked beside the gas pump I'd just left. As I pulled in behind the car, the driver was swiping his credit card in that gas pump. I ran over to him and began apologizing for my mistake. I told him I'd parked my car at that gas pump just minutes earlier, then mistakenly drove away without pumping my fuel after paying the clerk.

The fellow looked amused and could see I was telling the truth. This made sense because his credit card wasn't being accepted by the gas pump. The machine still had my $20 credit in it. Before relocating to another gas pump, he told me not to tell this story to my wife.

I pulled my car forward to the gas pump and began pumping fuel. When the gas meter finished at $20, I returned the nozzle to the gas pump, screwed my gas cap on, and drove away. Chuckling about my mistake, I couldn't recall anyone else ever doing this. To this day I've never heard of anyone paying for gasoline at a gas station and then driving away without pumping the gas into the vehicle.

Publish Your Book

It is now possible for any person to write a book and get that book published for free. Amazon has made this possible. I'm going to describe here how you can do this.

Turn your computer on and do a web search for kdp.amazon.com. This will bring up a Kindle Direct Printing web page which is part of Amazon Publishing. Before pushing the button to create a new account, have a cell phone with you that is turned on. It doesn't have to be your cell phone. Now push the new account button. The computer will ask for some basic information and then send a security code number to your cell phone. Put that security code in your computer and send it back. The computer will immediately send your cell phone another security code number. Put that second code in your computer and send it back. Now your computer will tell you that you have an authorized KDP account. With your chosen username and password, you can now access your KDP account anytime without going through any more phone security checks.

The next step to publishing your book is to fill out a couple of pages of information in your KDP account. This isn't difficult and doesn't take long. After you've done this, you'll be asked to download your book into the Kindle Direct Printing system.

At this point you'll be stalled until your book is finished and typed. If you're not familiar with typing a WORD document on your computer and saving it to OneDrive, have someone show you how this is done. It isn't difficult. When your book is finished, typed, edited, and saved on OneDrive, you're now ready to download your book into Kindle Direct Printing from your KDP account.

Here's where many writers will be stopped because this will require some computer skills. If you're not a savvy computer person, which I'm not, get help from a relative or friend who knows computers. My brother helped me. Give that helper your KDP username and password and they can access your KDP account from their computer. They can then download your book into Kindle Direct Printing using the Kindle format.

After this is done, your next step is to answer another couple of pages of questions in your KDP account. This doesn't take long and includes some banking information for book sales. Your book can be published as a paperback, hardcover, eBook, or any combination. You can publish in black and white or with colored pictures. The sales price for your book(s) is your choice.

Now your computer assistant needs to design a front and back book cover using Kindle's format. Book covers don't need to be fancy. When this is done, your book is ready to publish. Your computer helper can now push the publish button in your KDP account. Employees at Amazon will receive your book and review it for suitable content. Within a few days your book will show up for sale on the Amazon book website. Being the author, you can now go into your KDP account and purchase copies of your book(s) for a discount price.

If you don't know a skilled computer person who can help download your book into Kindle, you can hire people to do this for you. Do a computer search for Kindle Direct Printing and there are lots of computer technicians who will provide this service for a fee. To get your book edited and downloaded into Kindle Direct Printing with a front and back book cover will cost less than $1000.

Generating sales for your book is something you will have to figure out. Amazon will publish your book for free and list it for sale on the Amazon book website, but marketing the book will be your challenge. There are lots of secondary book publishers around the country that specialize in doing this. Cost of marketing with these companies can range from $1500-4000.

Made in the USA
Las Vegas, NV
13 January 2024

84261875R00075